LIVING IN HOTELS

Acknowledgements

MY THANKS GO first and foremost to all my brothers and sisters, each of whom contributed comments and anecdotes that have enriched the book. In addition, Tony and also Gabrielle and Robin – who managed the Savoy and the Foley Arms at different periods – provided many interesting details about the hotels; Nicholas sent me the valuable stock of documents and photographs he had put aside before the Savoy was sold; and Heidi and Chris sent me scans of all the photographs they had collected for a family film.

Furthermore, my thanks go to the two friends who were the first to read the manuscript: my old schoolfriend Margaret Minett who still lives in Cheltenham and knew my family and the Savoy in former days; and Monica Arnold who could give a more objective appraisal, as she lives in Switzerland and knows neither the Savoy nor my family. The two women's warm encouragement spurred me on. Besides that, Margaret sent me information about local publishers and possible venues. I also owe particular thanks to my former Thames & Hudson colleague and friend, Emily Lane, who read and edited the manuscript with professional meticulousness.

Last but not least, I thank my husband, the writer Erhard von Büren, for his forbearance and also for his useful advice, particularly concerning the narrative structure of the book. And, of course, I am very grateful to my efficient publisher John Chandler of Hobnob Press: working with him has been a delight!

LIVING IN HOTELS

Brown's in London,
the Savoy in Cheltenham

A MEMOIR

HELEN WALLIMANN

THE HOBNOB PRESS

First published in the United Kingdom in 2022

by The Hobnob Press
8 Lock Warehouse
Severn Road, Gloucester GL1 2GA
www.hobnobpress.co.uk

British Library Cataloguing in Publication Data
A catalogue record for this book is available from the British Library

ISBN 978-1-914407-37-6

Typeset in Adobe Garamond Pro 11/14 pt.
Typesetting and origination by John Chandler

Contents

Introduction

F ROM MY EARLIEST INFANCY I had always lived in hotels: from 1942 to 1945 at Brown's Hotel in London, and from November 1945 until 1963, when I started work in London, at the Savoy Hotel in Cheltenham.

The book begins with a brief account of how my father, who grew up in a rural village in Central Switzerland, became the manager of one of London's most prestigious hotels, and how he and his growing family lived through the war years in London. Here, already, certain events are seen through the eyes of a child.

The largest section of the book is devoted to life at the Savoy Hotel in Cheltenham during the years from 1945 to the 1960s.

We never had a private apartment in the hotel, nor did our rooms have private bathrooms. We had no more privacy than the guests. As my mother, with six children, could not keep an eye on all of us all the time, we enjoyed considerable freedom, both in the garden and in the hotel. As a result, we came into regular contact with an unusually wide range of people. We were in

The Savoy Hotel in 1939. As can be seen from the lettering just beneath the frieze, it was still a 'private hotel' (i.e. not licensed to sell alcohol).

daily contact with the staff: dishwashers, porters, chambermaids, waiters and waitresses, gardeners, housekeepers and office staff. We knew several of them quite well, saw them at work and sometimes helped them. So we knew their jobs, just as we knew how our father earned his living. Besides the staff, we knew the guests, especially the many long-stay residents whom we saw daily. We observed them with interest and were sometimes amused by their peculiar habits. They often chatted with us – most people like little children – and sometimes even gave us presents.

For this account, I have relied largely on my own memories of childhood and adolescence. However, I have also included information I had from my parents (verbally, from diaries and letters and from the memoirs they wrote for their children) and from my brothers and sisters. I found information about many of our hotel residents and staff in electoral registers and indexes of wills and administrations, census returns, newspaper articles, ship passenger lists, and in the internet in general. Most of the photographs come from the Savoy Hotel archives or from collections left behind by my parents.

1
How my Father became a Hotelier

Antecedents

I T WAS LARGELY DUE to the Great Depression and to his father's connections that my father became a hotelier. To understand how this came about, it is necessary to know something about my grandparents.

The Hotel Rigi-First in 1896 with the little train station where, some years later, my grandparents first met. (Photo signed M Stalder. Archives of the Rhaetian Railway.)

My paternal grandfather, Anton Wallimann (b.1870), came from Alpnach, then a village of less than two thousand inhabitants, near Lake Lucerne at the foot of Mount Pilatus in central Switzerland. The fourteenth of fifteen children, he was the only one to benefit from a secondary school education. After his six years at the village primary school, he was sent to a *collège* in the French-speaking part of Switzerland where he learned to speak and write in French. Afterwards he went to Italy to learn Italian. It was there that he found his first hotel job, as a porter. Later he went to England to learn

English, and there, too, he found work as a porter – at the London Savoy. Eventually he was promoted to *caviste* – in charge of the wine cellar.

Now fluent in four languages, my grandfather returned to Switzerland, where he became head hall porter (*concierge*) in two luxury hotels: Hotel Rigi-First[1] on Mount Rigi near Lucerne during the summer season, and the Suvretta House Hotel in St Moritz in the winter. Both hotels belonged to Anton Sebastian Bon, the founder of the Bon hotel dynasty that would, in 1928, buy Brown's Hotel in London.

Suvretta House Hotel, St Moritz, 1913. (suvrettahouse.ch)

One of the concierge's duties was to meet guests arriving by train at the Rigi-First train station. It was on one such occasion that he first saw my grandmother, Marie Schmid. Originally from the Grisons, she was the eldest of the three daughters of a minor civil servant who worked for the National Parliament in Bern. Her father died young without leaving a pension, and the family struggled to make ends meet. When Marie was eighteen and had just finished commercial school her mother died too. But with a diploma in her pocket the young girl was in a position to earn enough money to help at least one of her sisters finish senior school. However, the youngest girl left school at fifteen to go to work.

Later, Marie found employment as the station mistress cum postmistress at the Rigi-First Station – where she also found her husband. They married in 1906.

1 *First* is the German word for 'ridge, summit, peak'.

Alpnach-Dorf - Schulhaus

The new school building in Alpnach at its inauguration in 1916. This is the school my father attended before going on to the commercial school in Lucerne. (Courtesy Otto Camenzind, Alpnach OW, Switzerland)

From Country Lad to Banker

MY FATHER, Anton Paul Wallimann,[1] was born in 1908 in Alpnach. He was the second of three children. In spite of my grandfather's profession, my father was not expected to go into the hotel business. He liked to tell us how he grew up as a country boy, and how lovely it was to be able to go barefoot all summer, and how he hated having to put on shoes to go to Mass on Sundays. However, his mother was not a simple country girl: the daughter of a middle-class family, she'd grown up in Bern, the Swiss capital, and had had a good secondary education at a commercial school. She had higher ambitions for her children.

So, after primary school in Alpnach, my father went to the *Handelsschule* in Lucerne (near enough to commute by train), from which he graduated with a commercial diploma. He went on to a two-and-a half-year apprenticeship at the Swiss Credit Bank[2] that he completed in February 1929. Now he wanted to go out into the wider world. So two months later he took a train to Paris where – with excellent references from the Swiss Credit Bank – he immediately found employment as a trainee in the financial analysis department of a private bank. There he learned how to trade in the stock market.

1   The name is correctly written with two Ns. My father eliminated the second N before the war so as not to be taken for a German.
2   Now Credit Suisse.

At that time, it was almost impossible for foreigners in France to obtain a work permit. My father had none, and was thus working illegally. So when one day in November 1929 his room neighbour told him that the police had come and made enquiries about him, he thought it best to disappear. He fled to Brussels, where he was able to share a room with an old school friend. There he easily obtained a work permit. But because all the banks were laying off staff due to the Wall Street Crash, the only job he found was as a shorthand typist for German and French correspondence in the Brussels branch of the Opel Automobile Company. He worked there for four months and seized the opportunity to learn to drive a car.

Meanwhile, his father, who was during the winter season working as concierge at the Suvretta House Hotel in St Moritz, had had a chat with an English banker who was staying there as a guest. The man promised that he could arrange for Anton to be taken on by his bank in Lombard Street, London. So, in April 1930, off the young man went to England.

While waiting for his work permit to come through, he took a course to brush up his English. But what he didn't know then was that it was impossible for the bank to procure a work permit: due to the precarious economic situation they were already reducing their English staff, so the engagement of a foreigner could hardly be justified.

That was the end of my father's banking career.

The Beginnings of a Hotel Career

ONCE AGAIN MY GRANDFATHER, with his good connections, came to the rescue: a Mr Bieri, the former manager of the Hotel Rigi-First where my grandfather regularly worked during the summer season, had been promoted to manage Brown's Hotel in London after it had been bought by the Bon family. My father went to see him, and was successful: Mr Bieri who knew he could get a work permit thanks to an exchange with an Englishman working in Switzerland, agreed to employ him, provided that he promised to take up the hotel business as a career. My father agreed, and in August 1930 he took up the job at a salary of 35 shillings a week, half of which went on rent and bus fares. (He had a room with a family in SE 23, an hour's bus ride from Piccadilly. Later he was given a room in the hotel – so that he could work even longer hours!) He enjoyed the job, and stayed there until the end of May 1932 having, according to his testimonial, had 'a comprehensive training in all branches of hotel work including: Goods Receiving office, Dispense, Wine Cellar, Service, Internal Audit, Manager's Assistant'.

Brown's Hotel.

Now he felt he needed experience in other hotels. So he moved back to Switzerland, where he worked for various first-class hotels in all kinds of jobs (except in the kitchen – he never learned to cook). In the meantime, Mr Bieri's health had declined. He wrote to ask my father to come back to Brown's as his assistant – he had managed to get him a temporary work permit. So my father returned to London.

After working as assistant manager at Brown's for three years (from February 1934 to September 1937), my father was offered the job of 'saving the Prince of Wales Hotel and the Broadwalk Hotel in

THE PRINCE OF WALES HOTEL

DE VERE GARDENS, KENSINGTON, HYDE PARK, LONDON, W.

For Home Comforts and Cuisine unsurpassed. Accommodation for 140 Visitors.

THE PRINCE OF WALES HOTEL, W.

Situation most fashionable and central for pleasure and business, nearly opposite Kensington Palace and Gardens, quiet, being just off the High Street, Kensington, near the Albert Hall, within a few minutes' ride of Hyde Park Corner.

THE PRINCE OF WALES HOTEL, W.

Terms, inclusive, en pension, weekly, single, £2 12s. 6d. and upwards. Special reductions to families and officers.

Single Bedrooms . . . . . 4s. od.
Breakfast . . . . . . 2s. od.
Luncheon 2s. 6d
Dinner . . . . . . 3s. 6d.
Or daily, with full board and baths from 9s. od.

Address Manager—

THE PRINCE OF WALES HOTEL,

DE VERE GARDENS, KENSINGTON, LONDON, W.

Advertisement for the Prince of Wales Hotel, date unknown.

Kensington from bankruptcy'.[1] He was happy to be in a position to accept: on 11 May 1937, the day before the coronation of King George VI, he had finally received an unconditional work permit.

1   Quotation from my father's memoirs. The two hotels, owned by the same proprietor, were opposite each other, and about two hundred yards from Kensington Gardens. During the war, the Broadwalk Hotel would be requisitioned to house refugees from Malta.

The two hotels combined had 185 rooms. The clientele consisted mainly of long-staying residents. However, thanks to various improvements like brightening up the lounge furniture and introducing really good afternoon teas, my father attracted many new clients and managed to increase trade by forty per cent within twelve months.[1]

Family Matters

B Y THAT TIME, my father was nearly thirty years old – and still single. According to his own account, what with his long working hours, and having to keep a certain, professional, distance from staff and guests, he had become a lonely man. Now that he had a fine job, he felt it would be really nice to have a wife. He would have liked to find a Swiss woman, but as he could only go to Switzerland once a year on a two-week holiday there was no time to make the necessary acquaintances. So he asked his parents to keep a look-out.

My grandmother was happy to help her beloved son find a suitable, preferably Catholic, girl. It so happened that she knew that one of her friends had several as yet unmarried nieces. I knew my grandmother and her friend, who would become my great-aunt; so I can imagine the conversation they might have had.

'How's Anton getting on in London?'

'Oh, very well indeed. He's the manager of a leading London hotel now. A very good job. But he works so hard, poor fellow. He really needs a wife, a nice Swiss girl. But how can he possibly find one when he can only come home once a year, and that only for a fortnight? Do you happen to know anyone?'

'Let me think. What about my niece, Gritli Räber? You must know her family, the printers and book publishers, very well-known and respected in Lucerne. Don't you read *Das Vaterland*?'

'Yes, from time to time.'

'Well, they're the printers.'

Wedding of Anton Wallimann and Margrit Räber, January 1939.

1   According to my father's memoirs.

My great-aunt would have gone on to describe the young woman in the most favourable terms: how she was a trained bookseller who used to work in the family bookshop and help her father in the office. How she stayed at home to look after her dying mother, and was now running the household for her bereaved father. How pretty she still was at nearly thirty. That she could speak English, having been an au pair in England, and a family help for her brother's family in New York. And also that she played the violin.

'The violin? What a coincidence! Anton also learned to play the violin.'

Eminently respectable, English-speaking, Catholic, cultured and capable of running a household! What more could you want?

The match-making was successful. The couple corresponded, met, and got engaged in August. In November my mother and her sister Tini went to London to see what life would be like at the Prince of Wales Hotel. On 7 January 1939 my parents married in Lucerne. After a skiing holiday in Braunwald they returned to London.

The Phoney War and the Blitz

M Y MOTHER BRIGHTENED UP the hotel – and my father. She took him out to the cinema, to concerts (they heard Pablo Casals), and even to the opera. She lent a hand here and there in the hotel and noticed – better than my father – where renovation was necessary.

That summer, while my parents were on holiday in Switzerland, my father received a telegram telling him that war was imminent and that he should return to London immediately. However he was advised to leave my pregnant mother in Switzerland: all mothers and children had been instructed to leave London because bombs and gas attacks were expected.

But there were no attacks – it was the Phoney War. So just before Christmas, two months after the birth of my brother Tony, my mother with the baby took the train to Paris, where she had to go from pillar to post and fill in forms and pay something here and something there, but finally managed to book a flight to Hendon on the following morning. However they couldn't leave till the late afternoon, as the plane before them had had to return after being attacked over the Channel. So it was dark by the time they landed in Hendon. They were driven through the blackout to Victoria Station where my father was anxiously waiting to take them home to the hotel. It was the day before Christmas Eve.

The war still seemed far away and life went on as usual – until the start of the Blitz on 15 August 1940. The raids were intense. According to the diary my parents kept there was hardly a night without an alarm (that sometimes

Living through the Blitz. (Mirror, 9 April 2015)

lasted eight or nine hours) and they spent many a night in the shelter. They didn't sleep well and grew very tired. At first the bombs fell mainly on the East End and on the City. But in September they started falling on the West End too. The hotel was often shaken by the explosions. On the 10th and 11th bombs fell on Exhibition Road and on the Natural History Museum, only half a mile away. On the 12th my parents' parish church was burnt down. On the 19th there was only one alarm, at eight in the morning – a rest, like a real holiday, my parents wrote in the diary they kept of the bombings. But on the 20th shrapnel broke through two glass roofs of the hotel, and the following night an incendiary bomb fell on Kensington Palace. On 7 October, the hotel windows in the basement and on the fifth floor were shattered, stones from the pavement flew up as far as the first floor. On the 11th there was a flare outside the luggage room, but my father, who'd been firewatching, rushed down in his Minimax fire helmet and managed to put it out with the extinguisher, so that there was no damage besides broken windows. Subsequently the guests held a collection in support of the voluntary fire guards.[1]

1   My father had arranged a rota of fire guards, two at a time, among the staff. Because they were not available before the end of their duties in the hotel, he kept watch before that on his own. In his diary he wrote: 'At that time such a fire-watch was considered exceptional and I had extra arrivals just because of it. After half the city had burned, firewatching became compulsory.'

My mother was now about six months pregnant, but she decided to stay on in London until 22 October so that she and my father could celebrate Tony's first birthday together. On the 23rd she and Tony took the train to Neath in Wales, where they had Swiss friends who could put them up. On 13 February 1941 I was born there amidst the noise of German bombers and British anti-aircraft guns (according to my mother). My father managed to come for my christening a few days later.

Raids continued, in London,[1] but also on nearby Swansea. My mother was anxious to return to Kensington. On 8 April we were all back at the Prince of Wales Hotel.

My first stay in a hotel would last no longer than a week.

1   See Appendix.

2
How we survived the War

Difficult Times

I DON'T REMEMBER my first hotel, the Prince of Wales in Kensington. After all, I was only two months old when our stay came to an abrupt end: in the night of 16 to 17 April a land mine, floating on a parachute, exploded in Gloucester Road, wrecking sixteen houses. The Prince of Wales was the first building left standing, but the damage was great: doors ripped out with their frames, windows all broken, the plaster from walls and ceilings all down. My mother had been in bed, with me in a wicker pram beside her. She wrote in her memoirs that there was a terrible din and that she heard herself screaming at the top of her voice. She scrambled out from beneath the door that had fallen on top of her, and immediately switched on the light to see what had happened – only to hear an enraged street warden call, 'Lights out! Lights out at once!' She switched off the light, but not before she had ascertained that I was uninjured: the pram was full of glass splinters, but it had been pulled away from the door by the blast and had come to a stop in front of the wardrobe (the only one in that part of the hotel that had not toppled over, according to my father). Tony, who had been sleeping next door, was fine too, sitting up in his cot, rather dazed, playing with the rubble that had fallen from the walls and the ceiling. Meanwhile, my father had arrived. He'd been at the top of the fifth-floor staircase at the time of the explosion. The building shook so violently that he tumbled down to the next floor, and a skylight came crashing down on top of him. But his tin helmet saved him from injury. He was terribly worried that his family might have been hit and rushed down through the rubble to their rooms on the first floor. What a relief to find them safe and sound!

My mother always maintained that our family had been saved due to the intercession of the patron saint of Switzerland, Nicholas of Flüe. He was from Sachseln, which, like my father's birthplace, Alpnach, is in the canton of Obwalden, so he might well have had a soft spot for us. Be that as it may, when my second brother was born, just after the war, he was baptised Nicholas.

No one in the hotel had been injured. But our rooms, wrecked and without windows or shutters, were uninhabitable. What could be done?

My father rang the Candrians at Brown's Hotel (Albert Candrian,[1] a Swiss, was the manager; Helen Candrian was my godmother) and asked if my mother and the two children could stay for a few days until something had been arranged. They agreed, and we stayed for a week, while heavy raids continued. Then we moved to Hatfield, twenty miles north of London, where rooms were available in a large house the Swiss community had rented to accommodate residents from a Swiss old people's home in London that had been destroyed in the Blitz. In her memoirs, my mother wrote that it was 'a very nice house with a big garden and woods'.[2]

The family in Hatfield, 1941.

In spite of all the damage, the Prince of Wales Hotel still had electricity and water. My father decided to keep it open, although only about twenty of the seventy guests remained. He went to the Town Hall for help. He sat on the stairs until the Town Clerk arrived, and managed to persuade him to send twenty-four men to clear the debris and do the most urgent repairs: in

1   For further information about the Candrian and Bon families, search 'Suvretta-House: Familiengeschichte'.
2   In 1942, in the light of fuel shortages, the government gave permission for thirty-four of the trees to be chopped down and used as firewood. Swiss volunteers did the work.

'Westfield' in Hatfield, 1942. The manageress with me, Tony and a dog.

that way the hotel would not close, he argued, and the rates would continue to be paid.

Then, four weeks later, the patched-up Prince of Wales Hotel was bombed again, this time blasting the other side. My father still managed to keep it open. But when, in September, he received an offer from the Park Lane Hotel in Piccadilly to be assistant manager there, he was glad to accept. However, it was not at all as he'd expected, and after seven months he handed in his notice.

He found a new job as manager of an American Red Cross service club for soldiers on leave. It was to be set up in the Washington Hotel in Curzon Street, Mayfair, that had been badly damaged by bombs. So the first thing my father had to do was help as best he could to get the place repaired in time for General Eisenhower to open it as the 'George Washington Club' on 4 July 1942.

Meanwhile, my mother, Tony and I were still in Hatfield. We stayed there as paying guests for a year and a half. For although the Blitz as such was officially over by 11 May 1941, more than a million houses and flats had been damaged or destroyed. It was impossible to find lodgings for a family in central London.

Being separated from her husband for so long was a trying time for my mother, although she was kept busy looking after two children, sewing and knitting, helping in the garden, picking berries and looking after the hens. After a while she found a nice reliable girl, the daughter of a local farmer, to look after her children so that she could occasionally go to London for a day or two to see her husband. But, being an alien, every time she wanted to leave Hatfield she had to go in person to the local police station to obtain permission – an hour's walk across Hatfield Park to get there, and another hour back. Then, as soon as she arrived in London she had to inform the nearest police station that she was spending the night at my father's address. The following afternoon she would take a Greenline Bus to Barnet, where she had to change and find the right bus stop in a country lane (no names because of the war), and then, after the ride, walk for half an hour through woods and lanes. She had to be in by 10.30 or 11.30 pm, depending on which constable had granted the permission.

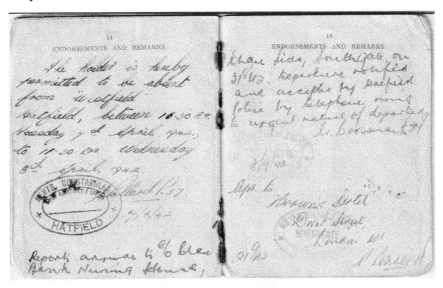

My mother's certification of registration. Transcription of the first entry: 'The holder is hereby permitted to be absent from "Westfield" Hatfield, between 11.30 p.m. Tuesday 7th April 1942, to 11.30 p.m. Wednesday 8th April, 1942, Herts. Constabulary Hatfield, 7/4/42.' The second entry refers to her going to the nursing home to give birth to Heidi: 'Reports arrival to c/o Chase Bank Nursing Home, Chase Side, Southgate, on 3/8/42. Departure notified and accepted by Hatfield Police by telephone owing to urgent nature of departure by U.Crossman.' The third registers the move to Brown's Hotel on 21/9/42.

Meanwhile, my father soon found his job at the American service club impossible: there were too many people from the Red Cross giving different instructions, ordering food without informing him, etc. So he gave in his notice and joined the family in Hatfield. He thought he could look after us two children while our mother was giving birth to the new baby that was expected within a month. But then the family managed to engage Miss Mary Simmen, a forty-year-old Swiss governess, to take care of us. We all liked her and she was to be our nanny until 1946.

At about this time, Mr Anton Bon,[1] the chairman of Brown's Hotel, came to the rescue: he was looking for a replacement for Mr Candrian (the manager of Brown's), who had caught tuberculosis and had to return to Switzerland. My father was delighted to accept the post.

That was on 7 September 1942, two days before the birth of my sister Heidi. As soon as my mother was strong enough, we all moved from Hatfield to Brown's where we stayed until the end of the war.

At Brown's Hotel

I HAVE FRAGMENTARY MEMORIES of our time at Brown's. I remember a sudden moment of joy when, after a walk with Miss Mary in Green Park through the cold, damp, darkening fog, we arrived home to find Mummy serenely sewing under the warm glow of a lamp. I remember admiring my father's bravery when he had to climb through a window up on the fifth floor to rescue me after I'd locked myself into the toilet.

I used to be delighted when the sirens went. It meant that we could go down to our lovely air-raid shelter! We'd rush into the corridor and ring for the lift. When it arrived, several people also got in, and the one-legged liftboy would be in a tizzy because he knew there would be people waiting on every floor and the lift wasn't big enough, so he'd whizz past and we'd arrive in the basement in record time. I have a very clear recollection of our cosy private room in the

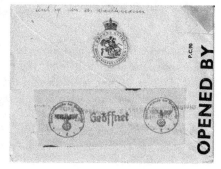

Letter examined by the British censors.   *Same letter examined by the German Wehrmacht.*

1   Anton Bon was the eldest son of Anton Sebastian Bon (d.1915), the founder of the Bon hotel dynasty.

air-raid shelter, of its wonderful three-tier bunk bed with a ladder and little curtains you could close. Tony slept on the top bunk and Heidi at the bottom. I considered my bunk in the middle to be the best, since you could use the ladder to climb into it, it had curtains, and you were not blinded by the electric light.

The shelter had been prepared for the exiled King Zog of Albania, his Queen Consort and their infant son, Crown Prince Skander. In 1941 the King had expressed an interest to move to Brown's from the Ritz, but then he changed his mind

In front of Brown's Hotel, early 1944.

and decided to move out of dangerous London, so the room wasn't used until we arrived.

As children, we were not aware that we were living in a luxury hotel. I remember being filled with wonder and delight by the Easter nest filled with little chocolate eggs that was created for us by the hotel patissier: the nest looked as if it had been built of thin twigs but, miraculously, it was edible (it was made of potatoes). Another culinary marvel was my fourth-birthday cake that was sprinkled all over with hundreds-and-thousands.

That might have been fine for children, but during the war it was difficult for the hotel to provide guests with the kind of meals they expected. They were not allowed meals of more

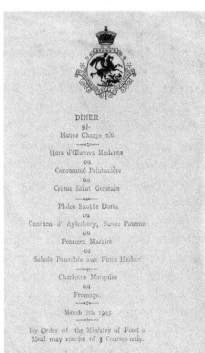

Diner menu at Brown's Hotel, 1945.

Barrage balloons over Central London.

than three courses (see 'Diner menu', p. 25). Besides that, according to my father, rationing allowed for only a pennyworth of meat per person per main meal. With luck, it might be possible to buy six chickens at the controlled price – on condition you took a hundred pigeons at about five times the normal price.

Once, my father managed to buy rabbits at the controlled price from a farmer from Kings Lynn, but the man charged as much again for freight. This was illegal and the man was apprehended and taken to court with my father as a witness. The judge was a customer at Brown's, and on seeing my father he smiled knowingly. The farmer was fined, but not my father, who was equally guilty. The next time the judge was at the hotel, my father asked him the reason. The judge answered that London was struggling so much to get food that no proceedings were taken against Londoners.

Another problem, according to my father, was that all kinds of things like towels or cutlery were pilfered. So he had to introduce a special routine: at teatime, each waiter received one teaspoon that was passed from one guest to the next and collected after everyone had stirred their tea. So even guests at Brown's suffered some hardship during the war!

To come back to my personal memories: I remember the pelicans in St James's Park. And, in Green Park, the 'feather man' whose coat was stuck full of feathers and who wore several hats one on top of the other; and the lady who drank methylated spirits, which made her act strangely and turned her face horribly blue; I remember how she screamed 'Get off my bench!' at a soldier who wanted to sit down next to her, and how he jumped up in alarm – what a frightening woman, even scaring soldiers! I remember the enormous barrage balloons that Tony called big Easter bunnies.[1] And also how clouds of acrid smoke from damp autumn bonfires incited us to put on our gas masks to see if they really worked. I'll never forget the man we saw sitting on top of one of the pillars of the park gates, who'd been up there for hours and hours, who'd even slept up there, and whose photograph was in the newspaper the following day – it was the first time I'd seen with my own eyes something so important that it appeared in the papers!

I also remember waiting with Heidi in the hotel staircase to see a princess (the Princess Royal?) come out of the room where she'd attended a meeting. To our disappointment, instead of wearing a little crown and a beautiful frilly dress, she was dressed in drab uniform!

'Mickey Mouse' child's gas mask provided by the British government in WW2.

Other important people who might have impressed us had we been older were the captains who came to celebrate their sinking of the German battleship *Scharnhorst*. Or Gromyko, the Russian ambassador to the United States, who called in. Or else Professor Gerbrandy, the Dutch Prime Minister, or Haile Selassie, the Emperor of Abyssinia, who both lived at Brown's during their exile.

We were so young that we'd never known anything else but war. It seemed to be normal. We never actually witnessed anyone being hurt or killed, and I can't remember ever being frightened. Nevertheless, the final year of the war had been very gruelling for Londoners, what with the V-1s – called doodlebugs – and then the V-2s. (My mother used to say that one of Heidi's first words was 'doodlebug'.)

Then at last the war was over – VE, Victory in Europe! In his memoirs my father wrote: 'Everybody went mad. Piccadilly was blocked to car traffic. We walked through the middle, ten in a line, arm in arm, singing at the tops of our voices. Then we went to Buckingham Palace and shouted with all the others: We want the King!'

I was too young to join the crowds. But we celebrated in our own special way: Miss Mary had lived in America for several years, so she was used

1   According to a letter my mother wrote to her family in October 1942.

to ticker tape. We were given old telephone directories and told to tear the pages into strips that we were allowed to throw out of the windows. Perhaps we were the only ones in London to celebrate in that way! Anyway, our parents soon stopped us. But I always imagined I'd seen Mr Churchill making his V for Victory sign – a sign that became common currency among children my age for many a year. Of course we probably did notice something of the celebrations, as Brown's is very near Piccadilly.

Apparently, my mother had been in correspondence with a French prisoner of war in Poland during the conflict, for shortly after VE day she received, from Paris, the following letter dated 9 June1945:[1]

Dear Mrs Walliman,

I am extremely happy to inform you that I am back home with my family. It's impossible to describe our joy. Words cannot express my emotion.

I arrived here yesterday morning after an eight-day journey in open cattle trains. It was very trying. But the main thing is that I have arrived safely. My arrival coincided with the announcement of victory, a good omen, don't you think?

But what about you, dear Madame, how are you? And your family to whom I send my kindest regards. I imagine that there is much jubilation among you too, now that the war is over. The end of the nightmare, what joy! Now I'm trying to recuperate, trying to forget all the horrors I experienced.

Toward the end of February we were evacuated from Görlitz,[2] forcibly of course, so as not to fall into the hands of the Russians. We covered nearly 800 km on foot. We were fed whenever it pleased those fine German gentlemen – and often we lay down with empty bellies after a thirty-kilometre march. We were guarded by sentinels who knew no pity, blows with rifle butts frequently rained down upon us. If I describe these details it is to give you an idea of what those good Germans who call themselves civilised were like.

We arrived in Helmstadt, which is 120 km from Hanover. There we had to work for the railways. On 1 April we were liberated by the Americans, and 25 days later I was back in Paris with my aged parents who, alas, are greatly changed.

Now I shall get myself demobilised and try to find my way back into

1   My translation.
2   Site of the prisoner-of-war camp Stalag VIII-A, on the Polish/German border. (See www.discovergoerlitz.com/stalag/) Belgian and French prisoners arrived there after the German invasion of France. It is estimated that 120,000 POW soldiers passed through the camp. Those below the rank of corporal were assigned to work on farms and in factories around Görlitz. One of the French prisoners was the famous composer Olivier Messiaen.

civilian life. I'm a radio salesman. And if one day I find a woman willing to have me – I'm no longer young, nearly 39 – I'll get married.

Before closing this letter I want to thank you for all the kindnesses you showed me. […]

Sincerely yours,

Henri Perkol

Monsieur Marin, a Frenchman, who came to replace my father as manager of Brown's at the beginning of September 1945, had also been a prisoner of war.[1] Previously he'd been the manager of the Dorchester (that also belonged to the Bon dynasty), but had been called up at the outbreak of the war. He was captured in Dunkirk and spent the rest of the war as a prisoner. I admired him. He was tall and handsome and spoke English with an enchanting French accent. A real hero!

'Why didn't Daddy fight in the war?' I asked my big brother.

'He couldn't. Because he wears glasses. They might get broken in a fight. Then glass could get into his eyes and he'd go blind.'

A truly shocking idea, and a convincing answer.

Interlude in Switzerland

WE LEFT BROWN'S HOTEL at the end of September, but couldn't move into the Savoy in Cheltenham as planned, because the solicitors were very short-handed and the formalities had not been completed on time. So we moved into the Montana Hotel, near Gloucester Road Underground Station. My parents had heard that Swissair had started flying one plane a week from London to Switzerland. After great efforts they managed to reserve seats for my pregnant mother, her three children and Miss Mary on the third plane to fly. My father remained in London to chivvy the solicitors.

I don't remember leaving Brown's. But I do remember the room we occupied at the Montana. It held an immense wardrobe, so big you could go in one door, creep through the clothes hanging there in the dark, and come out through another door. I also remember not being allowed to be sick in a paper bag in the airplane, but having to use a tin supplied by Miss Mary who didn't trust the solidity of the paper.

Then there was our arrival in Lucerne, with Tante Tini running down the road to meet our taxi as we drove up the Museggstrasse to the Musegghof where my maternal grandfather and many members of my mother's vast

1   The 1942 Restoration of Pre-War Practices Act stipulated that returning soldiers had to be given back their previous jobs.

extended family lived. I was impressed by the great welcome, and also by the banisters in the staircase that had been entwined with ivy in our honour.

Later, we taught our little cousins how to cadge chewing-gum from the GIs who came up the Museggstrasse on their way to visit the Town Wall and its towers. The phrase we taught our cousins was 'Any gum chum?' – we were convinced that Americans spoke slang and that 'chum' was American slang for 'friend'. We were very successful – to the dismay of our adult relatives.

US soldiers in Switzerland, 1945. (Souvenir book with 200 photographs published in Zurich in 1946.)

I remember our grandfather who called us *Miini drü müsli* (my three little mice); and our two great-aunts, Tante Marie and Tante Andett, in whose flat on the top floor of the Musegghof Heidi and I slept. They were so delighted each time we responded to their good-night incantation *Gelobt sei Jesus Christus!* (Praised be Jesus Christ!) with *In Ewigkeit, amen* (For ever and ever, amen) that they gave us sweets, although we'd already cleaned our teeth.

There are also some more troubling memories. Some days after visiting an emaciated old great-uncle on his death-bed, I complained that I wasn't feeling well. Then one of my legs was suddenly seized in a cramp that was so extreme and painful that I couldn't put my foot on the ground. It might have been a coincidence, but this happened while my mother was in the nursing home about to give birth to Nicholas. Of course everyone was alarmed and a great fuss was made of me. A lovely doctor was called and I hopped around the table on one leg to demonstrate the problem. He prescribed rest and hot poultices. I received lots of loving attention, and the next time the doctor came to see me I could run around the table in a normal fashion – to everyone's relief.

I also remember my brother Tony bringing home a box in the shape of a toadstool that he'd decorated at the kindergarten – where, he told me, they didn't do anything proper like the reading and sums he'd had at school in London with his teacher Mr White. Tony rather looked down on the other boys at his kindergarten: They wouldn't start school until they were seven, and they wore short trousers over long knitted stockings that were attached with garters to a bodice worn under their pullovers – really soppy!

I don't remember seeing our new brother Nicholas, nor the return flight to England with Heidi and Tony and Miss Mary, and our arrival in Cheltenham on 29 November 1945. I don't remember what it was like seeing Daddy again or what I thought of our rooms at the Savoy Hotel. Nor do I remember the arrival of my mother and baby Nicholas just before Christmas.

3
The Savoy Hotel

Before our Time

THE HOUSES in the stately tree-lined avenue named Bayshill Road were built in the first half of the nineteenth century when Cheltenham was at the height of its popularity as a spa. On one side of the road there are rows of terraced houses in the Regency style, and the Bayshill Road block of the Cheltenham Ladies' College, built in 1936 in the 'Cotswold idiom'.[1] On the other side of the road are several large villas designed in the Neoclassical style and set in spacious gardens.

Bayshill Road in 2020. The Savoy (now Malmaison) is the last building on the right.
(© 2022 Google)

The splendid house at the top of Bayshill is where I grew up. It was built in 1847 by Samuel Onley who had bought up much of the property of the Joint Bayshill Stock Company after it had gone bankrupt. Originally named Glenlee and privately inhabited, the building was expanded around 1880 and leased by the Cheltenham Ladies College from 1886 to 1901 to house 35 boarders.

1   https://historicengland.org.uk/listing/the-list/list-entry/1387848?section=official-list-entry

The new wing along Parabola Road was presumably added in the 1890s.[1] After the Ladies' College left, the house seems to have become a hotel. In 1912 it was sold by auction to a Mr T Curtis and became Curtis' Hotel. In 1915 Mr Curtis's plans for a new wing with a dining room were approved by the Town Council, so the present dining room may have been built around 1915/16. In

Villa with Ionic columns in Bayshill Road (Bryan Little, Cheltenham in Pictures, David & Charles, 1967. The photograph is not credited.)

The Savoy Hotel, late 1940s.

January 1924 the hotel was sold to Mr Frederick James Gregg, who submitted plans for additions to the building the same year. In 1926 he renamed it the Savoy Hotel.

In July 1942, the hotel was requisitioned for flight officers of the American 8th Air Force. They paid a weekly rent of four guineas a head and supplied the food. The hotel continued to be responsible for cooking and service. A month later, on 28 August 1942, Mr Gregg died, leaving his property to his sisters and to his brother, William. The latter was granted probate.

1   https://britishlistedbuildings.co.uk/101386741-savoy-hotel-and-attached-railings-cheltenham-lansdown-ward

The hotel viewed from the garden.

The hotel remained open. In 1944 the officers moved out, and by November it had opened for civilian guests.

The Savoy Hotel
CHELTENHAM

is now re-opened
for civilian guests

and invites enquiries for accommodation.
All bedrooms centrally heated and with gas fires.

Courtesy, Good Service and Comfort will be our aim.

Tel.: Cheltenham 2579

Notice in the Gloucestershire Echo on 14 June 1944.

The Hotel changes Hands[1]

WHILE MY FATHER was the manager of Brown's Hotel, he realised that London was not a suitable place for life with a young family. Besides that, he'd always had an urge to be his own master. He earned a good salary and by the end of the war he had amassed a nice sum of money. He had regularly invested savings in West End hotel shares and been very lucky that none of the hotels had been destroyed. Now he kept his eyes open for an opportunity to buy a hotel of his own.

It so happened that my father, being a good hotelier, was in the habit of receiving regular clients at the restaurant door and exchanging a few words with them. One of those regular clients was William Gregg, an old gentleman from Leatherhead. As he came to lunch about twice a week, the two men got to know each other quite well. One day Mr Gregg told my father that there was something he wanted to discuss with him. A date was arranged for lunch at Claridge's. Mr Gregg had also invited his solicitor, his banker, and a family friend. At one point in their conversation Mr Gregg said that he was a hotelier himself, and showed my father a picture of the Savoy Hotel in Cheltenham – without saying anything about it being for sale.

This intrigued my father, and a few days later he invited Mr Gregg to lunch in his private sitting room. Mr Gregg arrived as arranged and, even before taking a seat, announced,

'I want you to buy my hotel in Cheltenham.'

'Oh, thank you. Most thoughtful of you! But I don't even know where Cheltenham is. And I'm not sure that I could afford it. What price did you have in mind?'

'Never mind about that just now. Cheltenham's only about a hundred miles west of London. In the Cotswolds. Why don't you go there for a weekend with your wife? Then come and tell me what you think of it... By the way,' he added as an afterthought, 'I was thinking of about twenty-five thousand pounds.'

Shortly after this, my parents went to Cheltenham, taking Tony with them. Tony was particularly impressed by the 'mountainous' countryside: on the bus to Cleeve Hill, he kept everyone entertained by exclaiming again and again, 'Wow! Real mountains, just like Switzerland! Real, not just postcards!'

The Savoy Hotel was then unlicensed and full of old people. But my father saw that it had potential, and finally bought it for twenty thousand

1   The information in this section is from my father's memoirs.

pounds[1] that he managed to scrape together from his savings plus a mortgage and a six thousand-pound loan from the brother-in-law of another hotel client. (The brother-in-law laughed when the sum was mentioned – he wanted to invest in hotels, but he'd rather have dealt with sixty thousand!)

Tour of the Building

G UESTS ENTERED THE HOTEL up a few steps beneath a Classical porch, passed through the outer doors (open during the day) to a lobby with an antique oak seat on the left and an umbrella stand on the right, and on through beautiful bronze-framed brass-handled glass doors into the entrance hall. A barometer and maps of Cheltenham old and new hung from the walls. Opposite the entrance there was a fine staircase leading to the upper floors and flanked by a narrow passage. To the right there was a door leading to the lounge, to the left was a corridor. No reception desk in sight! Visitors had to turn left along the corridor to find it.

This was not ideal, so my father soon had everything reorganised. Next to the staircase there was now a new reception area with a desk opposite the hotel entrance to welcome arriving guests. The office behind the former reception desk had been moved to the next floor, leaving room for a little foyer with a couple of armchairs and a telephone cabin. The latter was essential because at the time there were no telephones in the guest rooms, only one in a first-floor corridor. If a call came in for a guest, the receptionist rang the corridor phone first, hoping that a chambermaid would hear it and notify the guest. If no one answered she sent the porter to summon the guest, who then took the call in the corridor or, for more privacy, came down to the phone box in the foyer.

The new reception desk.

When my father took over the hotel, it was 'centrally heated throughout' and all its forty-five

---

1   Worth about £920,000 in 2022. (Official Data Foundation/Alioth LLC)

A bedroom in the new wing

Another bedroom.

bedrooms were equipped with 'hot and cold running water, gas fires and rings'.[1] Only two had private bathrooms. Of course electricity had been installed long before, but on arrival my father removed 'miles of dead electric wires'. He also removed all the notices that Mr Gregg had hung up, including the one we children particularly took to heart: 'NEVER NEVER NEVER touch an electric switch with wet hands!!'

Although we were a family of eight (nine, counting the nanny), we never occupied more than five hotel rooms, all of them on the ground floor. The first of the two big rooms to the left of the entrance, facing south, served as a

For the convenience of Guests, an ELECTRIC SMOOTHING IRON is placed in the office and any Guest can have the use of it.

The charge is THREE-PENCE per hour, or part of an hour, if the current is taken off the "SPECIAL" supply.

If the current is taken off the "LIGHTING" supply, the price will be SEVEN-PENCE per hour, or part of an hour.

If any Guest uses any other Electric Iron, the charge will be 2/6 per hour.

One point must be clear, and there cannot be any controversy over this one point:-viz.

The time will be reckoned from the moment the Iron is taken out of the Office until it is handed back. If a Guest neglects to hand it back then the charge still will go on until such time as it is handed back.

If there is any friction over this point, then the iron will not be lent out any more.

One of Mr Gregg's notices.

bedroom for my parents and the two youngest children. The second became the children's living room, and at the same time a bedroom for Tony and me. Later, following the birth of Gabrielle, Nicholas moved in with Tony, and Heidi and I were given a bedroom of our own. Besides those three rooms, we had a sitting room for my parents and a bedroom for the mother's help.

In 1952, after we'd moved into the new house we'd had built in the far end of the hotel garden, the two big south-facing rooms would become the bar and the grill room; and our sitting room would become a room for meetings and private dinners (once even for a private dinner party with Princess Margaret).

The hotel lounge, much used by the many elderly residents, was spacious, bright and comfortable in an old-fashioned way. In the winter there was always a coal fire in at least one of the three marble fireplaces. There were large gilt mirrors above the fireplaces, silver candlesticks and cast iron figures of horsemen or shepherds and shepherdesses on the mantelpieces, and traditional pictures on the walls. There were lots of armchairs and sofas and coffee tables with ashtrays that we three older children used to empty every day while the guests were having their meal in the dining room. There were also two writing tables with inkwells, desk blotters, and paper and envelopes embossed with the hotel letterhead. These writing tables were often used, and we had to replenish them regularly with writing materials.

1   Hotel advertisements.

The lounge.

From the eastern side of the lounge you could go into the big bright conservatory[1] with its rattan armchairs and the overpowering smell of geraniums. Steps from there led straight into the garden... 'Secluded amidst three acres of beautiful garden' is how the hotel was described in the brochure.

However, in 1945 the garden was anything but beautiful. The former vegetable garden along Parabola Road was neglected and full of bottles and old boots, and half of the extensive main lawn was occupied by a waterlogged air-raid shelter. It was essential to restore the garden as quickly as possible. My father decided to attend to the main lawn first.

Around this time, he noticed that restoration work was beginning on the Cheltenham Imperial Gardens that had been used as an army campsite and lorry-park during the War. That gave him a bright idea that he put to the Town Council: they would be free to take the surplus soil from his garden instead of having it delivered from afar; in return, their men would level the ground so that turf could be laid. An agreement was reached and everything worked out well. Subsequently my father, together with William the gardener, got turf from a building site and recreated the big lawn. For years afterwards the pattern of turf squares was still visible, although William (and sometimes my father, aided by us children) regularly pushed or dragged a heavy roller over the uneven surface. Later, my father spent much of his spare time attending to the former

1   Presumably added in the 1870s. (https://britishlistedbuildings.co.uk/101386741-savoy-hotel-and-attached-railings-cheltenham-lansdown-ward)

The conservatory, presumably added in the 1870s.

The dining room, added by Mr Curtis 1916-17.

vegetable garden, providing it with trees and shrubs, a second lawn, a rockery, crazy paving, and a sandpit for the children.

The dining room could seat about seventy diners. It was high-ceilinged, with tall bay windows along one side. The walls were clad in splendid wallpaper that my sister Heidi and I found marvellously inspiring. It depicted a tiny couple sitting among majestic trees in vast, hilly countryside high above a lake. The same scene was repeated every few yards.

People usually came into the dining room from the lounge. The residents 'dressed for dinner', the ladies in long black dresses that hung desolately from shrivelled shoulders, the gentlemen limping in in their dinner jackets and black bow ties. As far as I can remember, there was one exception: Mr Howard, who always wore riding breeches.

Leading off from the dining room there was a small room that originally served as a smoking room for gentlemen. It had prints of Hogarth's *The Rake's Progress* hanging on the walls, and a bookcase with books that people thought you should own but didn't necessarily want to read, such as leather-bound sets of the complete works of Shakespeare, Thackeray and Kipling. There were also legacies from former guests, for example the 1894 edition of *Pocket Volume of Selections from The Poetical Works of Robert Browning* bought from A J Combridge & Co., Booksellers, Bombay, that contained the hand-written dedication: 'M Ollivant, With all good Easter Wishes – Bombay 10/4/98'. Judging by the numerous secondhand copies

Detail showing the wallpaper.

available nowadays on the internet, this must have been a very popular book with a wide distribution.

Later, the smoking room became the television room and then a room for private dinners.

What Guests don't see

Like the guests, we had all our meals in the dining room – except supper while we children were still small – and used the public toilets and bathrooms. This meant that we had the run of the hotel… We liked trying out all the toilets, and also going into rooms that were not open to guests.

For example, opposite our sitting room there was a small, dark storeroom where the handyman kept his tools, among them an enormous magnet. We used to spill all our mother's pins out onto the floor, then fetch the magnet to pick them up. It was magic! Also, on each floor there was a scullery that was used by the chambermaids. My mother used the one on the ground floor to wash the baby's nappies. It had a bell indicator panel with the room numbers that only popped open when a guest rang his/her bell. What a joy if you saw it happen!

Bell board similar to the one in the chambermaid's scullery.

A very important room that was inaccessible to the public was the stillroom or servery, from which waiters and waitresses collected the food to serve the guests. You reached it through a swing door behind the front staircase, below which a flight of stairs led down to the kitchen. As you entered

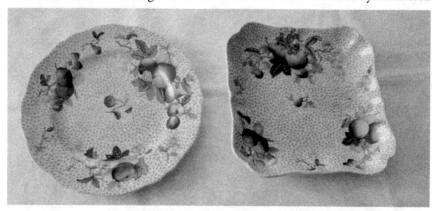

Plates from the china store.

by the swing door, you came into a passage lined with a narrow work table and cupboards. On your right there was the hand-operated dumb waiter that transported the food up from the kitchen when you pulled on a rope. In the stillroom proper there were gas rings with a grill against the wall on your left; and, also on your left, across the middle of the room, the stainless steel cabinet containing the bain-marie and hot cupboards to heat the plates and dishes. The bain-marie was gas-fired and contained water in which stood the pots of food that had to be kept warm. Behind these stood the cooks who took the waiters' and waitresses' orders.

The waiters and waitresses dumped the dirty plates and cutlery on a table in the hind part of the stillroom where the dishwasher worked. A nearby staircase led to an upper floor with four small rooms for live-in staff.

Diners could not see into the stillroom because there was a screen shielding the connecting swing doors – but sometimes they could hear the clanking of dishes and the shouting of orders. This made my father cross, and he would go and tell the staff to make less noise, please! Guests must never be disturbed, they had to be served without being made aware of their servants' efforts.

Beneath the stillroom there was the china store, that was only accessible from outside. It was full of new china that was kept in reserve, and there was also a lot of old china, some of which I'm still using today.

For us children, a more interesting part of the hotel was the basement beneath the new wing. It contained not only the wine cellar that was kept locked, but also another cellar that was always open. There we found great earthenware pots filled with eggs in limey water, lots of bric-a-brac, and, most fascinating of all, the statue of a naked woman, white and nearly life-size. There was also a large furniture store crammed full of beds and wardrobes, tables and night tables, chairs and armchairs.

Even better than the cellar was the attic between the two new wing floors. It was usually kept locked, so we could only go there when our father needed our help. We were still small enough to be able to walk upright there as long as we avoided the beams, whereas adults had to crawl, so we helped him take out the Christmas decorations, which included beautiful pre-war Chinese glass lanterns that would be hung over the central lights in the lounge and the entrance hall. At the end of the festive season, after Twelfth Night, we helped put everything away again.

It was also the place where old linen baskets, all kinds of large boxes, and the residents' trunks and suitcases were stored. We were fascinated by the stickers from all over the world. We found Mrs Clayton's suitcase, leather

Chinese lanterns.

with her initials embossed in gold on the lid. She was a lady we had known, small and elegant, with a tall, fat, fair-haired, adult son. They were both always impeccably dressed and had posh accents but said 'yis' instead of 'yes'. They had emigrated from South Africa after the death of Mr Clayton – or so they said. They stayed at the hotel for several weeks while waiting for the rest of their luggage and their money to arrive. Somehow their money never arrived and their bills had accumulated, so they had to leave. My father held back some of their luggage as a kind of guarantee. He also informed the police, who investigated and discovered that the Claytons were swindlers who had outstanding debts in many of the expensive shops in Cheltenham. So they were charged and, presumably, landed in prison. And we kept their luggage.

I remember trying on Mrs Clayton's wonderfully slinky silken nightdress in front of the mirror in our bedroom. I felt like a film star. As it was small enough for me I was allowed to keep it, although I was only ten. As to the suitcase, I used it much later when I went up to university in Edinburgh.

You could go down to the basement by a staircase just opposite our living room. We liked visiting Mrs Curtis in the linen room or Miss Elliott in the storeroom – where in 1945 my father had found mountains of peanut butter left behind by the Americans who had occupied the hotel during the War. (Unfortunately, he never found any chewing-gum.) There was also the so-called 'staff-room', with a long table and chairs down the middle, and shabby armchairs and sofas along the walls.

The kitchen was more or less out of bounds as it was considered both physically and morally dangerous for children: physically because of all the hot cooking that was going on, morally because chefs were renowned for their bad language. Actually, we were never tempted to go there, because it was hot and noisy, and we knew instinctively that we would only have been in the way, whereas the linen room and the storeroom were cosy places where we even felt that we could make ourselves useful.

When my father took over the hotel, one of the first things he had to do was convert the basement area – otherwise he would have had problems with the hygiene inspectors! A new kitchen was built beneath the dining room. It included the most frightening room in the whole hotel: the cold room. This was a walk-in refrigerator with a heavy insulated door that had only one handle so it could only be opened from the outside. It was all too easy to imagine oneself trapped inside and freezing to death! So I never dared go in.

The flagstone flooring in the basement was replaced by a cement floor in the corridor and tiles in the kitchen. My father told us that while the flagstones were being removed three men armed with kettles of boiling water stood ready for all the black beetles that came out. They'd been quite a plague, and I remember seeing them scuttle around. They had come with the anthracite that was used to stoke the boilers. The boilers were now removed to the basement beneath the conservatory, which was only accessible from the outside. The fuel was changed to coke, much later to oil and then to gas.

The new kitchen (1).

The new kitchen (2).

.I remember watching the kitchen porter wet-mop the basement floor. Before starting, he scattered damp tea leaves over the surface.

'Why do you do that?' I asked.

'It picks up the dust and the dirt,' he replied as he swept them into heaps. 'Look, do you see? Good, isn't it?' And indeed, it seemed quite efficient. However, the water in his mop bucket still got very dirty. And there were still a couple of those fearsome black beetles that had to be squashed.

Besides renovating the kitchen and redesigning the entrance lobby and reception desk, my father also had the dirty coffee-coloured camouflage that covered the building removed and the hotel façade painted creamy white. It was later floodlit in red, so that it could be seen from afar. Bit by bit, the hotel was re-carpeted throughout, rooms and corridors were repainted or repapered, new spring mattresses were provided for the beds, and the dining room and lounge were redecorated and refurnished. To my disappointment, the landscape-wallpaper in the dining room was replaced by one with a more conventional design.

One of our very special treats was when we were allowed to go up with my father on the hotel roof, a copper roof that had to be inspected for leaks. Of course, we never went on our own – except for Nicholas and Gabrielle, when they were still very small. Somehow they had managed to get out through a door that should have been kept locked, as it led to the roof that covered the new wing. The children were delighted to find themselves up there above the garden.

'Yoo-hoo, William, William, look where we are!' they shouted to the gardener who was working among the flowers.

He looked up in alarm: two small children sitting on the roof, their little feet projecting over the edge.

'Stay there, don't move!' he cried, and rushed into the hotel to alert my father, who immediately dashed upstairs, found the door still open and stepped very quietly out on to the roof so as not to alarm the children. There they were, very pleased with themselves, and sitting quite still, just as William had told them to. Not for nothing had we been called the best-behaved children in Cheltenham!

4
The Best-behaved Children in Cheltenham

'Thou shalt not be Noisy!'

IT WAS MRS BISSETT, the manageress of the municipal Information Bureau, who nominated us the best-behaved children in Cheltenham. Perhaps she was right: living as we did in a hotel, we had no choice but to be well-behaved.

As far as we were concerned, the First Commandment was: 'Thou shalt not be noisy.' And the second was: 'Thou shalt at all times show respect and consideration for guests.' It was the first that was the more difficult to obey, especially in the winter, when, inevitably, we spent more time indoors than in the summer.

The best-behaved children, 1949.

One game we thought suitably silent was hide and seek in the dark. We darkened our parents' bedroom by closing the inside shutters. Then, while one of us was counting to a hundred in the adjacent room, the rest of us hid. As the room was dark, we didn't really need to hide, we could simply lie without moving or giggling on or under a bed or on a table or a chest of drawers. We did try to hang Gabrielle, who was still very small, from the clothes hook on the back of the door, but luckily this didn't work. So we sat her in the sink. When the seeker came tension rose as they stumbled through the dark, feeling their way around until they touched someone. The child who had been touched had to be careful not to cry out, or it would be too easy for them to be identified. By the time everyone had been discovered, we'd usually had enough and no one wanted to have another round with another seeker. So we switched on the light and opened the shutters.

Heidi and I had a special quiet game we played once we had a bedroom to ourselves. We called it 'off-ground racing'. Starting simultaneously from our beds, we raced in opposite directions around the room, clambering over the furniture as best we could. The first to reach the other's bed without ever touching the floor won. The point where we met and had to cross over was particularly tricky, as was tackling the narrow windowsill. It was at this point that one of us once fell against the window and cracked a pane – the sash windows had very large panes. We went to bed quietly. The next morning we had breakfast before our parents were up, and went off to school as usual. At teatime, however, we felt compelled to confess. My father was very annoyed, particularly as he had notified the police that someone had tried to break into the hotel.

Our most common quiet occupation was, of course, reading or being read to. We borrowed books from the library, and Tony boasted of being able to read a whole book while walking home. We had our own books too, even Swiss books with lots of pictures like *Globi* and *Das lustige Männlein*. We also liked reading the comics that we exchanged with our school friends, especially *The Beano* and *The Dandy* but also *Hotspur* and *The Wizard* with their longer texts that I read simply for the pleasure of being able to, but found rather boring with their detailed descriptions of matches in which virtuous and courageous boys invariably won against cheats and cowards. Later we had subscriptions to *The Eagle* and *School Friend* which were more approved of by adults.

Otherwise we drew pictures, did picture puzzles, or played cards or board games like ludo, snakes and ladders, halma, or the Swiss (or German) game we knew as *Das Belagerungsspiel* (the Siege). We also liked playing with the black Bakelite model airplanes the American officers had left behind. Presumably they'd been used for aircraft recognition: they were streamlined

Favourite Swiss reading material: book featuring Globi, the most popular Swiss cartoon character.

The Dandy, Christmas 1947.

Also much loved: Das lustige Männlein (The Funny little Man).

and didn't contain details you wouldn't have been able to see from a distance. Our favourite was a Heinkel seaplane. Unfortunately it was the first model that broke, and in time they all went the way of so many toys.

We often worked on the stamp collection that my father had started while he was doing firewatching during the London Blitz. We had little packets of stamps and a *Stanley Gibbons Catalogue* that showed how much each stamp would be worth (theoretically) if we sold it. We were specialists on Swiss stamps that we received on letters from our relatives. We held the envelopes over steam to peel off the stamps which we then stuck into our album with others in the same series. Sometimes we managed to complete a series. Unfortunately, we never found any valuable stamps.

We had other activities too. We tried out things we found in a book we'd been given called *Things to Make and Do the Whole Year Through*. We cut out and assembled traditional Swiss houses from cardboard sets we'd received from our grandparents in Switzerland. These were kept on the mantelpiece together with the cage holding Tony's white mouse, Squeaker. Sometimes we let Squeaker out for a run on the mantelpiece where he liked to nibble

Bakelite recognition model similar to the seaplane left behind by the American servicemen who had been billeted in the hotel. (Le Comptoir de l'Aviation)

at the houses – he liked the glue and nibbled off many a chimney. We also gave him runs in the room, but once he got under the carpet and we had a panicky time worrying that we might inadvertently squash him. We didn't: we found him and put him back in his cage.

In the Garden

INDOORS WE HAD TO OBSERVE our First Commandment; being able to play outdoors was liberating. The hotel garden was spacious, with lawns big enough for croquet, tennis[1] and badminton, a rock garden, a small round pond, trees, bushes and high garden walls you could climb. We also had a swing and a sandpit. Occasionally a school friend or a child from the neighbourhood would come and play with us, but most often we were on our own. I particularly remember one neighbour with the delightful name of Susan Nightingale. She was older and very knowledgeable. It was she who gave me a convincing but puzzling explanation of how babies were born: through their mother's tummy button.

---

1   The brochure that Mr Gregg issued after buying Curtis' Hotel boasted a hard court as well as a grass court.

The big lawn with croquet hoops and deckchairs. In the background: Ladies College boarding house. On the left you see the rose walk.

Certain activities that we enjoyed required a lot of preparation. For example, if we wanted to turn the pond into a paddling pool we had to bail out the dirty water with buckets first, then clean away all the mud with rags

The east side of the hotel with the conservatory and the windows of the dining room. We sometimes played badminton on the lawn.

Watering the flowers in the hot summer of 1947.

and mops. After that we could turn on a tap and wait until the pond filled up with clean water. Then, if the weather had kept nice, we could put on our bathing suits and take the plunge. But if we splashed around too much the water got dirty again... Later, when we were living in our new house at the end of the garden, the cleaning process took much longer, because by then the pond was inhabited by countless newts, tiddlers and tadpoles. These had to be caught and carried upstairs to the bath that we had filled with dirty water and a few rocks to keep the animals happy while we used their pond. Surprisingly most of them survived.

Creating a badminton court on the smaller lawn outside the dining room was fun too. First you marked the lines, using a string stretched out between sticks you'd planted at each corner of the 'court'. Then you filled a special machine with a white paint you'd made from powder and water. After those preparations, you drew white lines by rolling the machine along the strings, trying not to wobble. Finally, you set up the net, and everything was ready for a game.

We had a very nice old croquet set that came with the hotel. The preparations for the game were simple. All we had to do was stick the pegs and the nine hoops into the lawn in the conventional pattern. As we had ten hoops, we always used two, one across the other, for the centre wicket, which gave you two points if you got through. Our lawns were never perfectly level – which sometimes gave poor players a chance.

We also liked playing in the rockery that my father had built. There were steps and paths and a little pool made out of an old sink. The rockery was very pretty, overgrown as it was with white rock cress and snow-in-summer, yellow basket-of-gold, grey-green Irish moss and blue and purple creeping phlox. My father had even planted some edelweiss, the Swiss national flower, but my mother maintained that it was not as white as that to be found in the Swiss alps. Gentians wouldn't grow.

In our Sunday best in the garden (1947). In the background: the cottage that would later be torn down to make way for our house.

There was another much bigger rockery in the pleasantly unkempt garden of a house on Parabola Road named Stoneleigh, a large mansion inhabited by an old gentleman who was very nice and allowed us to play there whenever we wanted to. Tony remembers that we played cowboys and Indians.

Unfortunately we had some gardening chores. The worst was weeding, especially the gravel paths. Picking up the twigs after my father had pruned the fruit trees was not quite as bad. Setting up deckchairs in sociable groups and putting them back in the sheds in the evenings was a bit of a bother, especially if the weather turned cold or it started raining and we had to put them away before they'd even been used. But we became expert at setting up and folding deckchairs without pinching our fingers.

We quite liked picking flowers for the tables in the dining room, or sweet peas that my father offered departing guests as buttonholes – until he noticed that the husband of a lady he was giving the posy to seemed to think he was flirting with her. Anyway, we preferred being taken out to the country to pick wild flowers to fill the hotel vases: to Cranham Woods for bluebells, or to some meadow for wild daffodils.

Besides having our own big garden, we could go and play in Montpellier Park that was only five minutes away. We took turns racing along the paths on our tricycle, one person pedalling, the other mounted behind. When we were a little older, we skated up and down the asphalt paths on our noisy, clamp-on, four-wheel roller skates, while elderly ladies and gentlemen – who'd expected to find peace and quiet in their local park – looked on disapprovingly and sometimes complained. And when we were old enough we played tennis that cost sixpence an hour for a hard court. We also liked going to Hatherley Park that had swings and roundabouts, and to Sandford Park for the lido. All those parks were within walking distance.

Useful Children

A S A YOUNG CHILD, the task I most enjoyed was helping my father collect the money from the guests' coin-in-slot gas meters. We'd go into each room and my father would open the padlock on the meter with a small key, slide out the money compartment and pour the coins into the bag I held ready. As we went from room to room the bag grew heavier and heavier. When we'd done all the rooms, Daddy poured the coins onto the middle of our big table and we children sorted the sixpences from the shillings then stacked them in piles of ten, two piles of shillings or four piles of sixpences making one pound. Finally, we added everything up, and it was a pleasure to see how much we'd 'earned'. Then my father would take the money to the nearby bank, together with the day's takings. He had a special little suitcase for all the coins, but he told us that he always stashed the notes and cheques into his breast pocket. In that way, if someone tried to rob him in the street, he wouldn't need to risk getting

Coin-in-slot domestic gas meter similar to the ones in the hotel guest rooms. (Museum of Applied Arts & Sciences, Sydney)

injured: he'd let them take the suitcase without a struggle. I thought that was an excellent idea!

Another very nice job was accompanying my father when he checked the guests' radiators at the beginning of the heating season. If a radiator wasn't hot he'd have to open the 'bleed valve' and a stream of air would rush out with a hiss. I'd be holding a small bowl under the valve to catch the jet of brown water that would suddenly follow.

A rather strange task that Tony had to perform from time to time was to play cards with the guests when someone was needed to make up a table during whist drives.

Once we'd reached secondary school age and had bicycles, we had a monthly job we called 'doing the cheques'. The tradesmen who supplied the hotel were paid by cheque on a monthly basis. My father had always dreamed of eventually having a chain of six hotels, one for each of his children. So he must have thought early training would be useful, and that addressing envelopes, writing out cheques and then delivering them would be a good introduction to one aspect of hotel management. When writing the addresses, you had to use 'Messrs.' or 'Esq.', depending on whether you were addressing a company or an individual. Thus, for our hardware suppliers we wrote

The local grocery owned by C.K. Fildes Esq. Now (2022) the Montpellier Wine Bar.

'Messrs. Sharpe & Fisher Ltd.', but Mr Fildes, the proprietor of our local grocery, had to be addressed as 'C. K. Fildes Esq.' When writing out the cheques you had to be very careful not to make a mistake and waste a cheque.

After our father had signed the cheques we put them in the envelopes, then set the envelopes in geographical order, making two or three piles, depending on how many of us would deliver them. Then we'd get on our bicycles and do our rounds. The shop assistants were invariably very nice to us. We always asked for a receipt. This was particularly interesting in the hardware store where they had a pneumatic tube system: the envelope was rolled up and inserted into a capsule that was then placed into a tube that sucked it up with a whooshing sound. You had to wait for a while before there was another whoosh and the capsule plopped out. The shop assistant unscrewed it and handed over the receipt.

The whole business kept us busy for half a day at least and saved my father a very small sum in postage.

We were paid sixpence each for this job. But we didn't usually bother much about money, or pocket money for that matter. If we needed something our parents gave it to us, and we made few demands: we were quite satisfied with the gifts we received for Christmas and birthdays, and also from Swiss relatives on a visit.

5
Special People, Special Times

Visitors

WE VERY MUCH ENJOYED the occasional visits from our Swiss relatives. First of all, it was our uncles or aunts who came. In those days you didn't fly from Switzerland to England for a long weekend. That would have been much too expensive, even if it had been possible. You took the train, and as it was a twenty-hour journey from Lucerne to Cheltenham you stayed for at least three weeks or a month.

My father had bought a car in about 1948 (after he'd hurt himself falling off his bicycle) and he loved taking our relatives around the Cotswolds to see the sights, so we children became very familiar with Gloucester Cathedral and Tewkesbury Abbey, the dry stone walls and the pretty Cotswold villages including our favourite, the Bourton-on-the-Water Model Village. Of course we always spoke Swiss-German with our relatives, and mostly with our nannies too, although they were meant to practise their English.

Nearly all of our twenty cousins were older than us, and several came to England to attend English courses. They were always welcome to stay with us, and were more fun than uncles and aunts, although they didn't usually bring us presents.

A Continental visitor who was not from Switzerland but from Austria turned up in 1948 and stayed in the hotel for three months. That was Fräulein Anni Danziger. She accompanied and was responsible for a hundred Austrian children who had come for a three-month stay with families in various parts of England. Sixteen of the children were put up in Cheltenham. I can remember how sorry we felt for them, knowing that they'd come because they didn't have enough food or clothes at home.

A British visitor we felt sorry for was a little girl from Nazareth House, the Catholic orphanage. My mother had arranged for her to come and play and have tea with us from time to time, perhaps because she had no relatives she could visit. We tried to be nice to her and to integrate her in our games,

Our first car, a Vauxhall. The photograph also shows, on both sides of porch, the 'iron balustrade of ornate panels with female masks' mentioned in the description in British Listed Buildings.

but I don't know if she enjoyed being with us. None of us really felt at ease – at least, that's how I remember it.

Visitors enlarged our horizons, but could also be a source of embarrassment, as was the case one Sunday when we were at Mass at St Gregory's with my Aunt Ada. Everything was as usual until the priest went up to the pulpit. According to his habit, before starting on his sermon he cast his eyes over the congregation. Suddenly he became agitated:

'You down there, cover your head!' he shouted.

Everyone looked around. Was there an unhatted, unveiled, un-headscarved female person in the church? My aunt looked up in alarm.

'Yes, you there,' the priest shouted. 'Where's your hat?'

Indeed, my aunt hadn't realised that girls and women were not allowed to go to church bareheaded – in this respect the Catholics in Switzerland were less old-fashioned than those in the English diaspora.

My aunt groped in her bag and found a crumpled little handkerchief that she put on top of her hair. I cringed in dismay. But the priest was satisfied and could proceed with his sermon.

Christmas at the Savoy

Years later one of those Swiss visitors, my cousin Othmar Schnyder, wrote to my parents:

One evening has remained unforgettable. It was Christmas or New Year [1951] when all your guests, many of whom were retirees, appeared at the festive dinner in formal evening dress. The gowns seemed almost as old as the ladies and hung despairingly from all too thin shoulders, while enormous decolletages revealed far too much wrinkly skin. Things got really bad for me when I had to play cards with two of those ladies and an elderly gentleman. I had no idea how to play, and all I understood of the ladies' well-meant advice was that they would kick me or prod me with a knee to let me know which card I should play. Well, I should have been filmed from under that table. I received a kick from the right, two from the left, then a prod from the right again, a kick and prod from the left – and this continued all evening, but I still hadn't a clue about how to play. I vowed there and then that I'd never ever again play cards whatever the game – a vow I have kept ever since.[1]

Unlike my cousin, I never played cards with the guests, but I loved Christmas. It was a busy time for all of us. We actually celebrated two kinds of Christmas, the 'real Christmas' and the 'hotel Christmas', and both had their charms.

The 'real Christmas' was of course our private family event, celebrated on Christmas Eve according to the tradition in Central Switzerland. Our parents' sitting room had been locked a couple of days before, in order to give the Christchild time to set up the Christmas tree and bring all the gifts. He would fly in and out of the room through a window that had been left slightly open for the purpose. At about four o'clock on Christmas Eve we put on our Sunday clothes, and then enjoyed a particularly good tea in our living room. After that we had to play very quietly so that we'd hear the tinkle of the Christchild's little bell that announced that everything was ready and that we could come. Even before reaching the door, we could smell the sweet scent of burning fir needles (a trick of my father's). As you entered the dark room, the first thing you saw was the Christmas tree, with its tinsel strips and intricate baubles glittering in the flickering light of the candles. On a small table beneath the tree there was a crib, with Joseph and Mary watching over Jesus in the manger, the ox and the ass, and the shepherds with a sheep or two. And all around on the floor, on chairs and on tables were the presents!

Before we pounced on our gifts we had to sing at least two Christmas carols: *Stille Nacht, heilige Nacht* and *Ihr Kinderlein kommet*. We sometimes also sang an English carol, perhaps *The First Nowell* or *Away in a Manger*.

1   Extract from a letter written in 1995 (my translation).

When we'd finished singing we were allowed to open our parcels and see what the Christchild had brought us. We could also start on one of the big boxes of chocolates we'd received from guests. Besides the chocolates, we enjoyed the special Christmas biscuits my mother had baked down in the hotel kitchen. She made three kinds: *Zimtsterne*, cinnamon stars made with whipped eggwhites, icing sugar, cinnamon and grated almonds; *Aniskräbeli*, aniseed biscuits, hard on the outside and soft in the middle; and *Mailänderli*, buttery biscuits that were shaped as stars, crescent moons and hearts and crosses, and hung from the Christmas tree. We used to help our mother cut out the *Mailänderli* with biscuit cutters and paint the shapes with egg yolk. The biscuits were then stored out of sight and we were not allowed to eat a single one before Christmas Eve.

We never helped decorate our own Christmas tree, as this was the Christchild's job. However, we were allowed to decorate the bigger one that was set up in the hotel lounge. We'd helped our father take the decorations from the new wing attic, and now we helped him hang the tinsel and the baubles. We made snow with little balls of cotton wool that we scattered around wherever we thought appropriate. A big sprig of mistletoe was hung in the doorway to the lounge, and we used to kiss beneath it – we always hoped we'd see guests kissing there too, but I can't remember that we ever did. The Chinese lanterns from the new wing attic had replaced the lampshades over the central lamps, and holly branches decorated picture frames and mantelpieces. Often this was holly we'd gathered in the countryside, always hunting for twigs with lots of berries.

We often made chains with strips of coloured paper stuck together with a paste made of flour and water. I can't remember that these were ever deemed worthy of being hung in public places, so we strung them up in our living room.

A few days before Christmas, our piano was moved into the lounge, and the tuner came to tune it – sometimes we watched him, and he explained what he was doing. This was in preparation for the Dixon Trio (Mr Dixon violin, Mrs Dixon piano and Master Dixon 'cello) that came every Christmas to give two or three concerts, mostly at tea time. We often attended and were allowed to sit in the very front, so that we could see everything.

In the letter quoted above, my cousin seemed only to remember the old residents. But actually quite a large number of 'ordinary guests' came to the hotel for the Christmas season with its special programme. On Christmas Day there was the traditional festive luncheon with turkey and Christmas pudding. The dining room had been appropriately decorated, and there were Caley's Christmas crackers on all the tables. We children had an important role to play: we were the animators! For once, we were allowed to – indeed had to – make a noise. So we pulled crackers, loudly used the whistles or squeakers that we found inside, and put on the paper hats. We also offered to pull crackers with Mr Winnall and Miss Span at the nearby tables. Other guests followed suit, so that by the time the chef came in with the Christmas pudding and set it alight, there was quite a joyful atmosphere.

After the guests had left the dining room, it was time for the staff Christmas meal. Tables were pushed together to make one long one. We decorated it with sprigs of holly and Christmas crackers, and after a while the staff members, dressed in their best clothes, took their seats. Now it was our turn to serve them. I remember it as a jolly event. But usually we'd hardly served the Christmas pudding when the first guests started ringing for their afternoon tea. No wonder I never wanted to go in for the hotel business!

Another highlight for us children was the conjuror's show. This took place in the lounge, in front of the fireplace nearest the dining room. The mirror above the mantelpiece had been covered with a cloth, so there was no risk of anyone being able to detect the magician's tricks. We sat on the floor at the feet of the guests in the front row of chairs and were invariably fascinated. Once, Tony was allowed to help the conjuror, but he didn't find out how the magic had worked.

When I was about nine or ten, I felt that we children should also provide some entertainment for the guests and that a nativity play would be just the thing. Tony wasn't interested, but I managed to engage Heidi, Nicholas and Gabrielle – Susy was too young, and she was also too wriggly to be of any use as a baby Jesus. We decided that the playpen, stood on its side and covered with a blanket, could serve as the stable. Gabrielle was the only one of us small enough to fit in, so she had to be Mary, and Nicholas, as Joseph, had to stand outside. Once that was decided, we set about dressing for our parts. By the time we were dressed up, Nicholas and Gabrielle had had enough, so all we managed in the end was the final tableau: a sullen Mary sitting in the playpen-stable with a doll on the floor in front of her, an impatient Joseph standing outside, Heidi and I, standing on chairs behind the playpen, representing the angelic choir. I held a violin to add to the realism. My mother and our nanny were suitably impressed, but we never got as far as a public performance.

Quarantine

C ELEBRATING CHRISTMAS among hotel guests and staff was an enjoyable time for us. But there were also times when we had to avoid all contact with guests and staff, when we were not allowed to roam through the hotel, not even to leave our rooms. Our meals were brought to us and we had to use chamber pots. It was then that we learned the meaning of the word 'quarantine'.

By 1945, the only illnesses infants were vaccinated against were smallpox and diphtheria, so contagious diseases that are almost forgotten today were still prevalent. In spite of our healthy lives and our regular intake of government supplied cod liver oil and orange juice we caught most of them.

In the autumn of 1946 we had chickenpox. In spring 1947, while my mother was at a nursing home giving birth to Gabrielle, we caught the whooping cough. Gabrielle received a vaccination before she was brought home, but I remember that we were

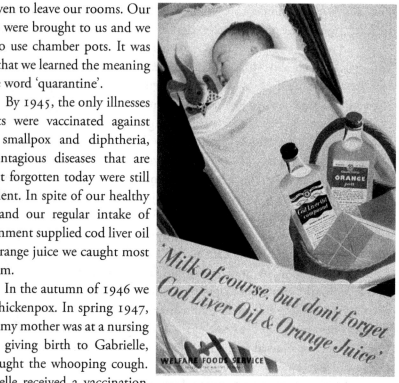

Government advertisement for cod liver oil and orange juice, issued by the Ministry of Food.

only allowed to see her through the front window. To soothe our lungs and throats, we had to do 'inhaling': a large bath towel covered the four of us as we bowed our heads over a bowl of hot water and inhaled the fumes of Vicks Vaporub. I found it very pleasant, but the others kept fidgeting, so the towel – which wasn't big enough – slipped and the experiment had to be broken off 'before someone gets scalded'. Instead, Vicks was now applied to our chests and covered with a layer of heated cottonwool held in place by rags and the *Seelenwärmer*. This was a triangular shawl that you wore over your shoulders with the two long ends drawn across your chest and buttoned behind your back. It really was 'soul-warming'.

In 1948 we all had the measles. A district nurse came regularly to give us penicillin injections that were so painful that the second time she came Nicholas locked himself in the sitting room and could not be persuaded to come out. Subsequently my mother said that she thought the nurse had been unnecessarily rough and asked our doctor to send a different one. After the measles, Heidi and Nicholas were so much weakened that Daddy took them to

Switzerland for a three-week stay in a children's convalescent home. Nicholas was only three at the time, so he probably doesn't remember much. But Heidi remembers being terribly homesick. Her only consolation was a lollipop Daddy had given her and that she kept in her handkerchief under her pillow: whenever she felt like crying she would give it a lick.

The last infectious disease we had while at the hotel was German measles in 1951, but that time only three of us were ill.

We were kept very strictly in quarantine, and I never heard of any of the guests or staff catching our diseases. But my mother must have felt relieved when we finally moved into our new house in April 1952. Living in a hotel with six children cannot be easy, especially when they all fall ill at the same time.

Mother's Helps

UNDER THE CIRCUMSTANCES, it was fortunate that my mother always had Swiss mothers' helps. They were older and could be given more responsibility than au-pairs. They generally stayed for six months to a year. Most of them wanted to learn English and attended language courses. But they usually spoke Swiss-German with us.

None of our friends had a nanny. Did we have one because we were Swiss? Or was it because we were rich? I knew we were rich because my classmate Maurice Green had told me so. He and Chris Lyons (who always had green snot coming out of his nose) sat behind me in class at St Gregory's. I loved and admired both boys, they were great fun.

'My dad says your dad must be very rich,' Maurice had said one day.

'Oh, why?'

'Because he's got five children… and a hotel!'

Well, many of my classmates had even more brothers and sisters than I did, and their fathers weren't rich. However, none of them lived in a hotel, so perhaps Maurice's dad was right.

The first nanny to come after Miss Mary left in 1947 was a cheerful, rosy-cheeked woman we addressed as Schwester (Sister) Rösi as she was a trained nurse. She was followed a year later by Fräulein Mathilde who was a singer and sang solo at concerts in Gloucester Cathedral and Cheltenham Town Hall. She wasn't very interested in us and only stayed about six months. Her successor was a treasure and we loved her. Her name was Marianne – yes, we were allowed to call her by her first name – and she stayed for a year.

The woman who followed was a trained child carer, so my parents thought it would be safe to leave us with her for a fortnight while they went to Switzerland on a winter holiday. However, when my parents came home, they discovered that she'd delegated all her tasks to me. I was only nine years old, but she let me bathe baby Susy in the sink in my parents' bedroom and change her nappies (using large safety pins) while she herself stayed in her room smoking and drinking. I also took Susy out in the pram. I looked after Gabrielle and Nicholas too, no doubt helped by Heidi and Tony. I felt very pleased with myself, but my parents were not amused and immediately dismissed the woman, whose name I have forgotten.

Then came Emma. She must have been a kindergarten teacher by profession, as she liked singing with us and taught us all the Swiss children's songs I know. We were very fond of her and were sorry when she left. But we also liked the woman who came next, a nurse from the Valais called Clary Perrig. What fun she was! She stayed with us for two years. Besides her English lessons she took riding lessons and promptly fell in love with her teacher.

Our last nanny, who came in about 1955, was Loni Wallimann, a distant cousin of my father's. She was more of a friend really, as we were getting too old for nannies.

6
Hotel Guests

Residents and Ordinary Guests

WHEN MY FATHER bought the Savoy at the end of 1945, the American officers who had been billeted in the hotel had left. The hotel had quickly filled up again, and my father took over an almost full house. In his memoirs he wrote: 'The whole country was then short of accommodation, so our occupancy was very high, yet a completely full house brought in only £50 a day. But then my wages bill was only £70 a week. [...] After the first year I saw that my income had doubled compared to what I had earned at Brown's.'

Basically, the hotel had two kinds of clients: permanent residents that we knew as 'the residents'; and 'ordinary guests' who came for shorter stays. In our first few years at the Savoy almost half of the forty-five rooms were occupied by residents, but gradually their numbers dwindled, decreasing from over thirty-five throughout the forties to only six or seven by the mid-sixties.[1]

Among the ordinary guests were businessmen and chartered accountants, parents visiting their children at one of the three public schools, motorists passing through (there were no motorways yet) and holidaymakers. People also came to Cheltenham for the horse races, especially the Gold Cup in March. In July, the Cheltenham Music Festival always attracted visitors, and sometimes the musicians stayed too. During the Cheltenham Cricket Festival we had county cricket teams staying. (Some of us used to collect the enamel badges from all the teams.) In October there was the Literature Festival, and in December, of course, the Christmas season with a special Christmas programme.

We hardly knew any of the ordinary guests, except for the few who came regularly. Occasionally we played croquet or badminton in the garden with holiday makers. I remember one occasion when we continued to play until it grew dark and one of the guests had to wave a white handkerchief over the hoops for them to be seen by the players. I found that very funny!

---

1   Information from the Electoral Registers 1937-72.

Unwelcome Guests

I HAVE ALREADY MENTIONED the mother and son from South Africa who stayed for several weeks at the hotel without paying their bills. They were an exception: in general, there didn't seem to be much criminal activity in and around the Savoy. Once a guest complained that jewellery had been stolen from her room. A police constable came to make enquiries. After interviewing the lady, he had a private conversation with my father. He showed him an album with photographs of past petty criminals. My father was rather shocked to recognise several former employees – the ones who had had gaps in their insurance payments, ostensibly due to illness, but perhaps really due to a term in prison. Anyway, there was no reason to suspect any of the present staff, so the policeman left. A couple of days later the case was solved: the guest had found her jewellery, that she'd put in a safe place and forgotten.

One evening, however, on 23 January 1947, we really did have a burglary. At about ten o'clock, the night porter saw a young soldier in uniform standing in front of our parents' bedroom, where Heidi and Nicholas were sleeping.

'What are you doing here?' he asked.

'There was no one around, so I couldn't ask. But isn't this Mrs Henderson's room?'

'No sir, you're mistaken,' answered the porter, who happened to know that Mrs Henderson had a grandson in the forces. 'But it is rather late, isn't it? Wait here, while I go and enquire if she can receive you.' And he went to our sitting room, just round the corner, to ask my parents if they thought he should go and inform Mrs Henderson of the visit, or if it wasn't too late. When he came back, the soldier had vanished.

A little later, on going to bed, my mother saw that a drawer and the handbag inside it were open and that several things were missing: a purse containing about three pounds, and three ration books for clothing. Of course she immediately informed the police. She was quite convinced that the soldier was the burglar.

And so it proved, for the following day he recidivated by stealing 'half a bottle of rum and half a bottle of sherry' from a house in Yarnold Terrace, Cheltenham. The day after that, he was apprehended by two policemen, but on the way to the Police Station he suddenly ran away. One of the officers followed him 'and was almost overtaking him when Teale [the burglar] drew a sheath knife from his clothing and clasped it in his right hand. Witness closed with Teale and Teale fell to the ground. In doing so, Teale had made a movement towards witness with the knife. Teale was overpowered and taken to the Police Station.'[1]

My mother had to testify before the court. There she recognised a bracelet the defendant had also stolen from her. She was shocked when she heard that the man had drawn a knife when the police tried to stop him running away – she couldn't help imagining what might have happened if Heidi (then aged four) or Nicholas (fourteen months) had woken up.

Celebrities

MY OLD SCHOOL FRIEND Jane remembers having tea with me in the lounge one day while Agatha Christie was staying at the hotel, and that we were so awed that we spoke in hushed tones. That must have been in the early 1950s. I don't know the purpose of Agatha Christie's visit or how long she stayed. Unfortunately, I've lost the autograph album that contained her signature.

Sir John Barbirolli, the famous conductor of the Hallé Orchestra, usually stayed when the orchestra was playing in Cheltenham during the Music Festival. My mother often chatted with him and later cherished a signed photograph he had given her as a souvenir. Usually several members of the Hallé Orchestra – which is based in Manchester – also lodged at the hotel.

Sir John Barbirolli (right) in the Festival Club, 1950s. (Cheltenham Spa Official Guide, undated)

A concert audience in the Music Festival of 1965. (Bryan Little, Cheltenham in Pictures, David & Charles, 1967)

1   Quoted from the *Gloucestershire Echo*, 3 February 1947.

On 1 November 1963 the Beatles performed at the Odeon Cinema in Cheltenham. They were booked to stay at the Savoy. Before their arrival, my father and the manager of the cinema hatched out a plan to get them safely to the hotel after the concert without a horde of screaming fans following them and disturbing all our guests. The plan was successful: while the Beatles' van, followed by the fans, drove off into the countryside, the Beatles themselves exited by a back door and were driven to a rear entrance of the hotel garden. From there they only had to walk along a garden path to get to the hotel, but it was dark and they turned towards our house by mistake. My sister Susy, who happened to be looking out of the window, saw them and showed them the way.

The next morning, they all signed Susy's autograph album. But she 'wasn't into pop music', so she sold George Harrison's autograph to a school friend for two shillings and sixpence. She doesn't know what happened to the album with the remaining three signatures – they'd be worth rather a lot of money today.

A few fans also managed to find the boys. Two girls came for a cup of tea in the lounge and waited long enough to catch their idols as they were leaving the hotel. Another girl met John and Ringo outside the hotel and asked them for their autographs. As she didn't have anything on her for them to sign, Ringo and John wrote on a scrap of paper that one of them found in his pocket – it contained the set list for the concert, handwritten by Paul McCartney, and is now apparently worth from £15,000 to £20,000.[1]

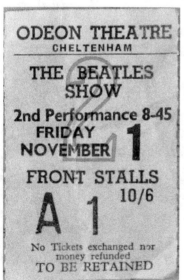

Rolling Stones ticket. (tracks.co.uk)

Beatles ticket. (gloucestershirelive.co.uk)

1   According to an organisation in the internet named We-Buy-Beatles.

The mayhem surrounding the event inspired the *Daily Mirror* reporter to coin the new term 'Beatlemania' which appeared in the newspaper's headline the following day: 'Beatlemania! It's happening everywhere... even in sedate Cheltenham'.[1] Later, the cinema manager told my father that after the Beatles gig he'd had to have all the seats dry-cleaned because so many fans had wet their pants in excitement.

It was probably the same after the Rolling Stones' gigs in 1964. The day after the performances, the *Gloucestershire Echo* reported:

The Odeon cinema where the concerts were held. (harveystevens.com)

Police officers, security men, commissionaires and first aid men linked arms last night to prevent screaming fans from rushing the stage at both performances by the Rolling Stones at the Odeon Cinema. One girl managed to clamber onto the platform, but was quickly hauled down. During their lively act the Stones were pelted with sweets and other objects as tokens of affection... After the show crowds of fans waited outside in front of the cinema, but the Rolling Stones slipped out the back way with a police escort and went off in their own car.[2]

1   https://www.mirror.co.uk/news/uk-news/the-beatles---unseen-pics-from-1962-424972
2   https://cheltenham4u.blogspot.com/2007/08/rolling-stones-tour-of-cheltenham.html

Unlike the Beatles, the Rolling Stones were not well-behaved hotel guests: apparently they had girls in and out of their rooms all night, and the following day the chambermaids complained that they'd left their rooms in a terrible state, and even a full chamber pot, uncovered and stinking, on one of the tables.

A few years later, the hotel welcomed a very different kind of musician, the celebrated pianist Alfred Brendel. He often performed at the Music Festival and usually stayed at the Savoy. Once, when he needed somewhere to practise, my sister Gabrielle's husband, Robin Pagan, had the honour of driving him round to a friend's rather splendid house in Christchurch Road, where there was a grand piano in a big airy room. Robin felt that his modest 60s Morris Minor was quite unsuitable for such a renowned person, but Brendel squeezed in and was thankful for the ride.

The Long-Stay Residents

> I imagined that I had to bring the saucepan to the boil, then turn off the gas and allow the egg to lie for three minutes in the cooling water. [...] To me, for whom meals had hitherto appeared as though by clockwork and the routine of a house had seemed to be worked by some invisible mechanism, the complications of sheer existence were nothing short of a revelation.[1]

SINCE THE FIRST World War, when factory jobs with regular hours and days off became available for women, those willing to go into domestic service with its irregular hours and restricted freedom became rare. The 'servant problem' was a frequent topic. And indeed, what were ladies to do without maids and cooks? Few knew how to cook or how to manage a household without the help of servants. Therefore they couldn't go on living in their draughty mansions with the beautiful high-ceilinged rooms, the many fireplaces, the traditional kitchens and antiquated plumbing, the big gardens. So the mansions were sold, and many genteel couples and single men and women 'of independent means' moved into hotels and guesthouses for the rest of their days. They were joined by others who had served His Majesty in the colonies and found themselves in the same predicament on their return to Britain.

Needless to say, the people could not take all their many possessions with them when they moved into a hotel. This resulted in some fascinating auctions where my parents bought several beautiful things, before antique dealers came

---

1   Vera Brittain, *Testament of Youth* (1933).

My parents at a fancy dress ball wearing garments they had bought at an auction.

My father in his attire as president of the Cheltenham Chamber of Commerce.

up from London and prices rose. I remember strange-shaped African gourds and intricately carved wooden boxes with mother-of-pearl intarsia. But the most remarkable objects were a brown-white-and-gold- striped djellaba woven in one piece; and a splendidly embroidered Chinese mandarin robe. My parents wore the garments at a fancy dress ball in the fifties when my father, as President of the Cheltenham Chamber of Commerce, was a member of the prize-awarding jury.[1] I also remember seeing at an auction some horrible examples of colonial booty: a rhinoceros horn, and a wastepaper basket made from an elephant's foot.

Cheltenham Spa – reputed for its mild climate that was said to be particularly suited for people recovering from tropical diseases – was a favourite choice for retirement. According to the Cheltenham Spa brochure for the 1951 Festival of Britain, the town had about forty hotels with a total of more than a thousand rooms offering full board and lodging at weekly rates per person ranging from 4 to 13 guineas (from 7 guineas at the Savoy). Besides that, there were at least a dozen guest houses with weekly rates between 3½ and 6 guineas.[2]

1   Both of these garments are now stored in the Ethnographic Museum, University of Zurich..
2   A guinea was 21 shillings. A pound was 20 shillings.

Very reasonable, one might think, but prices must be compared with the average weekly wage in 1953 which was £9 5s 11d for men and £5 0s 3d for women. By 1969, weekly rates at the Savoy Hotel started at 24 guineas for a single room with full board and 44 guineas for a double room. In the same year the average full-time male worker was paid £30 a week, while a female full-time worker earned just £16 6s 6d. As these are averages, many people – among them most of the people employed in hotels – earned less. And my own annual salary at that time, when I was working as an editorial assistant for a well-known book publisher in London, did not exceed £1,000, slightly more than the average female salary, but much less than the male salary! I certainly couldn't have afforded to reside in my father's hotel.

So most of the guests must have been very comfortably off – as is confirmed by the sums left by former Savoy residents listed in the *Index of Wills and Administrations*: in fourteen wills of residents who died in the 1950s and 1960s, the sums range from £3,950 to £75,800, giving an average of £27,730 equivalent in purchasing power to about £660,000 today (2022).[1] There is, of course, no indication of how the money had been invested. Presumably some of these people had received good dividends and some must also have had a pension. Nevertheless, occasionally there were indications that money was a problem, as the following anecdote illustrates.

One day, when we were already living in our house in the garden, my

A.A. ★★★   R.A.C. ★★★

SAVOY HOTEL
CHELTENHAM
SAVOY BAR—SAVOY GRILL

Telephone 0242 27788 (3 lines)

Tariff

Single Bedroom and Breakfast,			
	per day	from	55/-
Single Bedroom with Private Bedroom			
and Breakfast, per day		from	65/-
Double Bedroom and Breakfast,			
	per day	from	100/-
Double Bedroom with Private Bathroom			
and Breakfast, per day		from	110/-
Single Bedroom and Full Board,			
	per week	from	24 gns
Double Bedroom and Full Board,			
	per week	from	44 gns
Daily Rate, including full Board		from	75/-

(for a stay of not less than 3 days)

Full Board includes Breakfast, Lunch and Dinner

Terms for Children on application

Luncheon from 9/6   Afternoon Tea 6/-
Dinner from 17/6   or from 12/6 a la Carte
in Grillroom

Early Morning Tea 2/-   Coffee 2/-

Meals served in Bedrooms 2/- extra

Small dogs only allowed (not in public rooms),
5/- per day

Garage 3/6 per day   15/- per week

10% Service Charge

Also **Foley Arms Hotel**, Malvern Tel. Malvern 3397

June, 1969

Savoy Hotel tariff 1969.

1   https://www.officialdata.org

Bowls at Suffolk Square, less than ten minutes from the Savoy. (Cheltenham Spa Official Guide, Festival of Britain Edition, 1951)

The Promenade with the famous department store Cavendish House. (Cheltenham Spa Official Guide, Festival of Britain Edition, 1951)

*Shops for the upper classes in the Promenade, Ayris and Slade. (Advertisements in the
Cheltenham Spa Official Guide, Festival of Britain Edition, 1951)*

mother was called because of an emergency in the hotel: one of the residents
had apparently had a stroke. She immediately rushed to his side and, seeing
that he was conscious but very shaken, called out,

'Quick! A brandy!'

'Another five shillings on the bill! Oh no!' sighed the old gentleman,
closed his eyes and passed away.

At the end of 1945, when my father took over the hotel, there were
about thirty-five permanent residents living there. Their numbers would
remain almost stable for the next eight years and then gradually decrease until,
by the end of the sixties, there were only a handful.[1] In our eyes, the residents
were very old. Some of them had funny habits, but we were always polite
and respectful toward them, as we'd been taught. However if, as occasionally
happened, a lady wanted to kiss us, or asked us to kiss her powdered cheek
(how I hated that!), we were allowed to refuse by telling her that 'Daddy and
Mummy say we mustn't kiss people who're not in our family'.

1   Information from the Electoral Registers 1937-72.

Cheltenham racecourse.
(Cheltenham Spa Official Guide, Festival of Britain Edition, 1951)

Cotswold hounds meet in the Promenade. (Cheltenham Spa Official Guide, Festival of Britain Edition, 1951)

The Town Hall. (Cheltenham Spa Official Guide, Festival of Britain Edition, 1951)

Central spa in the Town Hall. (Cheltenham Spa Official Guide, Festival of Britain Edition, 1951)

Spa medical baths, the lounge. (Cheltenham Spa Official Guide, Festival of Britain Edition, 1951)

Because we saw them every day and often talked to them, we children felt we knew most of the guests quite well. But really, we knew very little about them – nothing about their former lives, and not much more about their present activities. Were they members of one of the clubs like the New Club and the Victory Club, or of one of the three bowling clubs? Did they go shopping in the Promenade? Did they play golf, go to the races, watch cricket matches, visit the Cotswold Hunt meet in the Promenade? Were they big readers? Did they go to the theatre? (I can't imagine that any of them ever went to the cinema.) Perhaps they went to concerts – or did they simply listen to the little orchestra that played each morning in the Town Hall while people took the waters? Did they use the spa medical baths? Or, in warm summer afternoons or evenings, did they watch the orchestra playing in the Imperial Gardens or in Montpellier Park?

A modern photograph of the bandstand in Montpellier Gardens, built in 1864, restored in 1994. (Brian Gibbs)

Certainly, they had some regular habits. Their days were structured by mealtimes: breakfast between 8 and 10, luncheon between 1 and 2 pm, dinner at 7. And every day they 'dressed for dinner', before congregating in the lounge to listen to the six o'clock news that boomed out from the enormous radio. If they'd missed it, they could listen to the nine o'clock news. After that, most of them retired to their bedrooms.

On sunny days, some of the residents sat out in the hotel garden. Occasionally they'd play cards at tables set up in the lounge for a whist drive.

Some residents spent quite a lot of their time in the lounge and came to regard it as a private sitting room, with their own private armchairs. One day, a visiting guest complained at the reception desk that when he'd wanted to take a seat in the lounge, an old lady tried to stop him by saying, 'You can't sit there, that's Miss Graham's chair.' The next day all the residents found a note from my father in their pigeonholes, informing them that seats in the lounge could not be reserved.

The Tatler, February 8 1950.

Judging by the papers left on the coffee tables (that we used to leaf through when we were emptying the ashtrays), some of the guests read the daily press, mainly *The Times*, the *Daily Telegraph*, the *Gloucestershire Echo*, and, very seldom, the *Daily Express*. They also read magazines like the *Sphere*,

Daily Express, December 8 1952.

Tatler, *Punch*, and occasionally *Horse and Hound*. We children were critical readers. We found *The Times* pretty useless: the only place you might find something worth reading was on the first page, in the personal columns. The *Daily Telegraph* was not much better, but at least there were some photographs. The *Gloucestershire Echo* was all right because it had local news. The *Daily Express* was good, with plenty of interesting short articles on the first page. As for the magazines, *Horse and Hound* only had pictures of dogs and horses, and the *Tatler* showed posh people and stately homes. However, we enjoyed the *Sphere* with its many really interesting pictures and *Punch* with its funny caricatures and jokes.

In general the guests were very kind to us. At Christmas we always received so many enormous boxes of chocolates that our mother made us pass some on to the Nazareth House children. One lady gave us a beautiful wax doll that was as big as a ten-month-old baby but wore old-fashioned girls' clothes. You could easily dress and undress her, as only the hands, the feet and the head were of wax. She had real blond hair and eyes that opened and closed. She was antique and rather fragile, so we were only allowed to play with her under our mother's supervision. We once managed to escape so that we could give the doll a haircut. That made my mother very cross.

One guest was a member of a jigsaw puzzle library. She sometimes lent us very big, really old, wooden puzzles after she'd done them. I remember one that showed a crowded street during a traffic jam that was caused by a confused old lady with an overloaded shopping bag standing in the way of a horse-drawn tram. That was very funny! But my mother always worried that we'd lose some of the pieces: you could never check if you still had them all without doing the puzzle all over again.

Several of the guests stayed at our hotel for many years. Their biographies reach back into the nineteenth century: Mr Lyall was named Hooker after his godfather, Joseph Dalton Hooker, said to have been Charles Darwin's closest friend; Miss Peatfield chose the subject of Klondyke for her fancy dress at a ball in 1898, the year the Gold Rush was at its height.

7
Remarkable Residents

I REMEMBER some of the guests quite clearly, can see them in my mind's eye, hear their voices. But for information about their lives, I had to do some research.

As I only knew the guests by their surnames, my first step was to consult the annual Electoral Registers, in which all those entitled to vote are listed according to their address at the time of registration. There I found the full names of all the guests residing at the Savoy in any given year. Having their full names, I could now look them up in the national censuses to find out their date and place of birth and their profession, together with the same information for each of the family members and servants living in the same household. Unfortunately, the most recent census I could consult was the one from 1911, since census records remain closed to the public until a hundred years after the date they were conducted. I found further information in indexes of births, marriages and deaths.

A very small number of guests featured in newspaper articles I found in the British Newspaper Archive. A few guests were in lists of ships' passengers entering and leaving the UK. Almost all the guests finally landed in the *England and Wales, National Index of Wills and Administrations*.

My personal memories of the guests together with biographical information might give an idea of the kinds of persons who lived in hotels in Britain in the 1940s and 1950s.

The Elegant Lady with the Quavery Voice

M RS CLIFT WAS, in my eyes, very old – she was seventy-three in 1948, when I first knew her. But she was still a true lady, so elegantly dressed and with such refined manners! Quite tall and slim, she might once have been described as willowy. Even at her age, she walked in such a graceful manner that, according to the hotel housekeeper, Miss Elliott, young men would follow her and then be disappointed when they reached her and saw how old she was. As she always wore a hat when she went out, they wouldn't have seen her tastefully tinted greyish-blue hair that was arranged in soft waves – unlike the tightly permed fashions of the time, or the grey buns other old ladies wore.

I remember her voice, wobbly and little-girlish when she asked for a pound's worth of sixpences at the hotel reception desk.

'For the one-armed bandit,' she explained.

'The one-armed bandit?'

'Yes, at the New Club, you know. He takes away all my money, heehee!'

Someone else she said took away her money was Fidel Castro,

Mrs Clift as a young woman.

in 1959, when he nationalised the Cuban sugar plantations in which she probably had shares.

'That naughty man, Mr Castro! He's stolen all my money!' she'd complain petulantly, but not quite seriously. After all, she still had enough money left over to pay her hotel bills – and to give Tony a gold half sovereign that he still treasures.

Eric H. Clift, 1916. Photograph on his Flying Certificate.

Mrs Clift was born Mary Lovell Simons in Jamaica in 1876. By 1881 she was living in England (at Beckenham in Kent). She had an older brother and sister, and then eight younger brothers. (Miss Elliott – who was surprisingly well-informed – told me that she'd been much spoiled by all her brothers who nicknamed her 'Puss'.) In 1898 she married Eric Hollocombe Clift, a civil engineer who worked 'on his own account'.

In 1911 Mr and Mrs Clift were living in Kensington with their eight-year-old daughter, Mr Clift's mother, and two female servants. In 1916 Mr Clift was awarded a flying certificate at the Beatty School, Hendon. Unlike other men who received a certificate around the same time, he had no military grade.

In 1921 the family were living in Poole where, according to the jury list, Mr Clift's 'Title, Quality, Calling or Business' was 'Gentleman'. He died in 1922, at the age of forty-eight.

In the following years, Mrs Clift lived with her daughter, who had remained single. A couple of years after the death of her daughter, in 1945, Mrs Clift moved to the Savoy. She was to stay there for twenty-six years until, in 1974, she moved to a nursing home. She died there two years later, at the age of 101.

The Lady who gave me a Dictionary

WHEN OUR FAMILY GREW too big for one dining-room table, two of us used to sit at a separate table next to the one occupied by Miss Span, a tall, thin, mild, old lady with a long face. She usually came in when we'd nearly finished our meal, and sometimes we stayed a little longer to chat with her. She always asked how we were getting on at school. When I started learning French she said that she loved French and had been to France when she was younger. Later, when I started reading literature for my A Levels, she gave me the 1928 edition of *Bellows' French Dictionary* that had been given to her in Tenby in 1929.

It's a very special dictionary. The layout of the lexical part is unconventional: the French-English and English-French vocabularies are not printed in separate sections of the book, but in separate sections of each page. Besides the lexical part, the dictionary contains all the grammar required for school French, as well as two coloured maps, one of the British Isles, the other of France and Switzerland. (Poor Belgium, that also has a French speaking population, was neglected.) It's very handy, being leather-bound and printed on paper so thin that the book is not even an inch thick in spite of its 680 pages. The dictionary, first published in London by Longmans in 1911, was a great success, and the 1928 edition in my possession was published simultaneously in London, Paris, Geneva and New York. It has recently been reprinted. The fact that the authors and printers of the book, John and William Bellows, were from Gloucester makes the dictionary particularly interesting for Cheltonians.

Miss Span would have been surprised – and perhaps pleased – to learn that I became a French teacher! And also that I have kept her dictionary all these years.

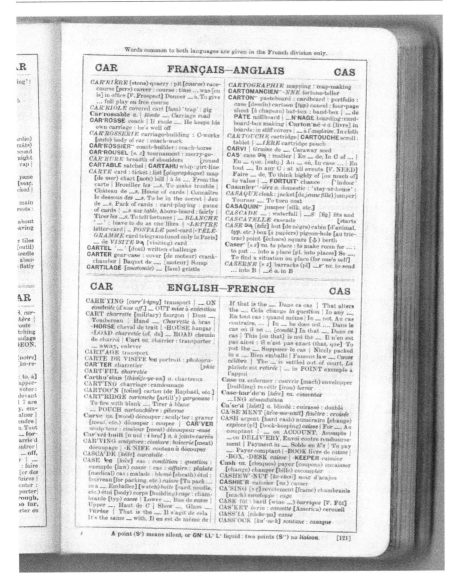

Bellows' dictionary.

Although I used to see Miss Span nearly every day, I knew very little about her, and know little more now. Her full name was Alice Ethel Span, and she was born in 1873 in India, where her father was a civil engineer in the army. She had four brothers, all born in India; three became army men and one studied theology. In 1881, according to the census, she was a 'scholar' staying with a widow and her daughter (both from India) in Shanklin, Hampshire. Later she lived with her parents in Tenby, South Wales. Her father died in 1917, aged about eighty-six. After her mother died, in 1926, Miss Span, now

aged fifty-six, moved into a hotel in Tenby. In 1947 she came to the Savoy –
her mother was from Gloucestershire – and lived there until her death in 1956
at the age of eighty-three.

The Modest Solicitor

I N THE DINING ROOM, Mr Winnall sat next to Miss Span. He was old and
didn't expect to live much longer.

'Oh, Mr Winnall,' my mother would say. 'Have you had a nice walk?
Not too cold for you?'

'Good afternoon, Mrs Walliman. Well, there is a nasty wind. A good
thing I had my good old winter coat on.'

'Old's the word Mr Winnall. Perhaps you should buy a new one? Your
overcoat looks rather worn out.'

'Just like me, Mrs Walliman, just like me. No, no, buying a new one
would be a waste of money. This one will do splendidly for the time being, I'm
not likely to survive the winter anyway.'

'You said that last year, Mr Winnall. But you survived and you don't
look any older than you did then. But your coat does. I don't know what
people think when they see one of our guests in such a worn-out coat.'

'Don't worry, Mrs Walliman. I'll buy a new one next winter – if I'm still
here.'

'Well, take care of yourself.'

'You too, Mrs Walliman. Goodbye for now.'

Although he didn't think he had much longer to live, Mr Winnall
still prepared himself for one of the disabilities of old age: my brother Tony
remembers him saying that he regularly practised reading Braille in case he lost
his sight.

Mr Winnall was already a resident at the Savoy when my father took
over the hotel in 1945. He was then aged eighty, so we children were right
when we thought he was very old. We liked him, but we knew nothing about
him. Even now, all I know is that he was born in 1865, his given names were
Charles Pears, he'd been a solicitor in Wales, had lived in Bournemouth after
his retirement, and had remained single all his life. He died in 1958 at the age
of ninety-three, after a brief stay at a nursing home. He left an estate of just
over £33,000.

A Man of Private Means

U P TO ABOUT the middle of the twentieth century, in the national census
the occupations of middle-class ladies tended to be registered as 'none',

'spinster', 'wife', 'unpaid domestic duties' or 'private means'. Gentlemen, on the other hand, always had some kind of profession: merchant, clerk of the Holy Orders, vicar, engineer, solicitor, colonial civil servant, Indian officer retired etc. Mr Lyall was an exception: his occupation was always given as 'private means'.

By the time we came to the Savoy in 1945 he was already a very longstanding resident: I found his name in the 1933 electoral register. He seems to have had no visible idiosyncrasies, for all I can remember about him is his roundish face and avuncular manner.

He was born William Hooker Lyall in Notting Hill, London in 1875, the third child, second son, of the Royal Navy surgeon and botanical explorer in Antarctica David Lyall.[1] He was named Hooker after his godfather, Joseph Dalton Hooker, one of the founders of geographical botany, and reputedly Charles Darwin's closest friend.

In 1878, when William was three years old and his father already retired, the family moved to Cheltenham. William attended Cheltenham College and then Oxford University. In the 1901 census – when he was twenty-six – and in all further records he is listed as living on his own means.

In August 1914, immediately after the outbreak of the First World War, Mr Lyall, then aged thirty-six, joined the army (6th Dragoon Guards). He fought in several battles in Belgium and the north of France, before being discharged in November 1915 with the rank of sergeant. He was later awarded an MBE. His brother, a Sandhurst-trained officer, had been killed in action in October 1914.

Mr Lyall never married. From about 1921 on, he lived in a house in The Park, Cheltenham, seemingly alone. He came to the Savoy in 1933, when he was fifty-eight, and remained there until his death twenty years later.

The Archdeacon's Widow

MRS SINCLAIR lived at the Savoy from about 1946 to 1948, so we were still quite young children when we knew her. She seemed very old, and also very old-fashioned: every week a horse-drawn carriage stopped in front of the hotel to take her for a ride. This fascinated us, and we would rush outside to take a good look at the horse and the coachman, whose name was Mr Bell.

1   There is an interesting article, 'David Lyall (1817-1895): Botanical explorer of Antarctica, New Zealand, the Arctic and North America', in *The Linnean*, 2010, vol. 26(2). It can be downloaded from the internet under www.antarctic-circle.org/stein66.pdf

One day Mrs Sinclair was kind enough to invite Tony and me to accompany her on her ride. How exciting! However, for me the outing started with a disappointment: my brother was allowed to sit out on the box with the coachman, but I, being a girl, had to take the seat inside the carriage with Mrs Sinclair. Tony still remembers the long whip the coachman so skilfully flipped at the horse to goad him on. All I can remember is the stuffy smell inside the coach.

Later, I learned that Mrs Sinclair's destination was the same every week: she took her laundry to Shurdington to be washed by her former housekeeper.

Bowden Hall in Upton St Leonard's, near Gloucester, the house in which Mrs Sinclair (Clara Sophia Birchall) was brought up.

Mrs Sinclair really was old in 1946: she'd been born Clara Sophia Birchall in 1862 in Harrogate, Yorkshire, the first child of a wealthy woollen cloth merchant. Her mother died the year after her birth. Later, the family moved to Upton St Leonards in Gloucestershire, where they lived in a house called Bowden Hall (now a hotel). They had nine servants: a governess, a footman, a page, a cook, a housemaid, a lady's maid, a laundress, a kitchen maid and an under-housemaid. Two gardeners and the groom lived with their families in houses on the Bowden estate.

In 1873 her father remarried. The family continued to live at the same address and eventually had four more children.

In 1893, when she was thirty-one, Clara Sophia married John S. Sinclair, a vicar in Fulham, London. He later became Archdeacon of Cirencester, and in 1901 the family was living in the vicarage there with their three small children and seven servants: a lady nurse, a nurse (domestic), a butler, a cook, two housemaids and a kitchen maid.

In 1909, the Archdeacon bought a mansion named The Greenway (now a hotel). In the 1911 census, he and his family were living there with their two daughters aged eleven and eight (their two sons, who were older, were probably at boarding school) and seven servants including a governess, a nurse and a footman.

The Greenway in Shurdington, near Cheltenham, where the Sinclairs lived from 1909 to 1919.

The Archdeacon died in 1919, and the house was sold.

Afterwards, his widow lived in Sussex, before moving to a house at 17 Priory Place, Cheltenham (a listed building since 1955), where she lived with three domestic servants. She then stayed at the Savoy for about two years before her death on 16 May 1948. She left her considerable fortune of £52,802[1] to her eldest son, who was Provost of Guildford Cathedral.

The Lively Lady with Intellectual Aspirations

MISS ANNIE PEATFIELD lived at the Savoy from 1946 until her death in 1951. I remember her only as a grandmotherly, unassuming woman. Her biography, sketchy as it is here, is probably very similar to that of many unmarried, upper middle-class women of the late nineteenth and early twentieth centuries. Yet Miss Peatfield seems to have been rather enterprising in her younger years, and had she been born only fifty or sixty years later, she might have benefited from opportunities that a spinster could only dream of in her day.

As it happens, Annie Peatfield was born in 1876 in Nottinghamshire. She had a sister, Alice, her senior by one year, and a younger brother named Charles Dickens Peatfield, who later became a surveyor. Their father was an army surgeon, and their mother, according to the 1881 census, a landowner.

By 1891, Mr Peatfield had retired, and the family was living in Cheltenham, in a house in Queen's Road. They had a relatively modest household with only two servants: a cook and a housemaid. The children were still 'scholars'.

By 1898, Annie and her sister Alice, both in their early twenties, had started going to the sumptuous balls that were held in the Assembly Rooms

1   Equal in purchasing power to over two million pounds in 2022. (https://www.officialdata.org)

The Assembly Rooms in the High Street at the corner of Rodney Road photographed in 1865. 'Although the exterior was somewhat austere and undistinguished, the ballroom was spacious and beautiful, and remained throughout the nineteenth century the centre of the town's social life. The Assembly Rooms were demolished in 1900 to make way for the present Lloyd's Bank.' (From Robert Beacham, Cheltenham as it was... a pictorial presentatiom, Hendon Publishing Co Ltd, 1976)

in Cheltenham. In January that year they attended the New Club Ball (accompanied by their parents). In February they were at the Cheltenham Bachelors' Fancy Dress Ball, with Annie as 'Undine' and Alice as 'Klondyke' – very topical as the Goldrush was then at its height, but was she dressed up as a prospector or as a saloon girl? According to the report in the *Cheltenham Chronicle,* the Fancy Dress Ball was 'one of the most brilliant yet known, eclipsing in gaiety and unflagging interest all its predecessors, and forming a fitting finale to one of the most successful seasons that Cheltenham has yet experienced'.[1]

In May of the same year, Annie took part in a Ladies' Bicycle Gymkhana in the Montpellier Gardens.[2] In 1899, the two young women attended the Ladies' Fancy Dress Ball, dressed as 'Pierrettes', Alice in white and Annie in black.

From time to time the family enjoyed seaside holidays: in the 1901 census the two daughters – now aged twenty-five and twenty-six, and still

1   For newspaper accounts of the balls see the Appendix.
2   For an account see the Appendix.

THE FOREMOST LADIES' PAPER

FIRST *in Interest* – FIRST *in Influence* – FIRST *in Fashions.*

THE . ILLUSTRATED . WEEKLY
JOURNAL . FOR . GENTLEWOMEN

PRICE SIXPENCE

BRIGHT READING BY THE BEST WRITERS
BRILLIANT ILLUSTRATIONS BY THE BEST ARTISTS

Scale of Charges for Advertisements.

The Measurement of Page is 14 in. by 9 in.

One Page	- - - - -	£30 0 0
Half Page	- - - - -	£15 0 0
One Column (4 Cols. to Page)	-	£7 10 0
Position Pages	- - - -	£35 0 0

Front Cover Page by special quotation.

These prices are subject to discount of 10 per cent. for
six insertions and 20 per cent. for 13 or more insertions.
Special rates for special numbers. Advertisements
must reach the office not later than FRIDAY,
1 o'clock, in the week preceding date of issue.

Offices : 70 and 76, LONG ACRE, W.C.

The Gentlewoman, 1910.

single – were in Hastings with their parents; and in 1903 they had a summer
holiday in Bournemouth, this time without their parents.[1]

By 1906 Alice, the elder of the two sisters, had stopped going to balls,
whereas Annie went to that year's Cheltenham Hospitals Ball and Cotswold
Ladies' Ball.[2] The following year, she again attended the Cotswold Ladies' Ball,[3]
and also the Badminton Club Ball.[4] After that there was no more ball-going:
at over thirty, both young ladies were now too old for the marriage market.

1   *Gloucestershire Echo*, 11 July 1903.
2   *Cheltenham Examiner*, 10 January 1906 and 17 January 1906.
3   *Cheltenham Examiner*, 16 January 1907.
4   *Cheltenham Looker-On*, 5 May 1907.

Annie engaged in other activities. She seems to have been a regular reader of *The Gentlewoman: An Illustrated Weekly Journal for Gentlewomen*, a periodical that existed from 1890 to 1926 and was reputed for its 'high tone and artistic and literary excellence'.[1] In the edition of 1 January 1910, Miss Annie Peatfield is named as one of some two hundred persons deserving an Honourable Mention for their contribution in a 'Picture Puzzle' competition. In February of the same year she had more luck and – deservedly in my opinion – won a thermos flask for the two alliterative truisms she submitted: 'Words without works are but waste; Works without wisdom are worthless. / Marriage minus means means misery; Means minus merriment make misanthropes.'

A year later Annie submitted an essay on Tariff Reform to a competition organised by the Cheltenham Women's Tariff Reform Association. Only five essays were submitted, but hers failed to win a prize.[2] Nevertheless, it shows that she was among the few women who took an interest in political questions.

Annie's parents both died in Cheltenham, her father in 1919 and her mother in 1928. Annie subsequently lived, without her sister, at hotels and guest houses in Cheltenham.

By 1946 she was living at the Savoy where she stayed until her death in 1951.

The Prince of Chess

Mr and Mrs Heathcote came to the Savoy in 1946. I see them in the dining room, sitting at their table in the bay window nearest the smoking room. Mrs Heathcote had to have a jug of hot water with her breakfast and also brown toast, white toast and brown bread. Mr Heathcote was a quiet man with a moustache.

I did not know then that he was famed as 'England's best composer of chess problems, and possibly one of the best the world has ever had'.[3]

He was born in Manchester, the son of a brewer. He was one of six children. The family were quite well off and employed a cook, a housemaid and a 'waitress'.

Godfrey became a solicitor. In 1897, at the age of twenty-seven, he married Mary Catherine Bayldon, the daughter of a general commission agent, in Wakefield Cathedral. The couple had two sons, both of whom went

1   *Truth*, 1898.
2   *Gloucestershire Echo*, 2 December 1911.
3   *Hastings & St Leonards Observer*, 4 January 1938.

to Malvern College. The older one, William, was killed in Ypres in 1917 at the age of eighteen. Their younger son, Ralph, joined the Royal Navy in 1919 and became a lieutenant commander, then a captain. He married, had a son, and, after his retirement, lived in Hornby, Lancashire.

By the 1911 census, Mr Heathcote was already retired, although he was only forty years old. He probably lived on the proceeds of his chess activities. He was well established in chess circles, as can be seen from the following extract from A C White's *Times* biography that was quoted in the *Falkirk Herald & Midland Counties Journal* on 17 May 1905:

> The work of Mr Heathcote may well be taken as the highest standard of problem composition to-day. It is first and foremost essentially modern. Mr Heathcote is absolute master of both two-move and three-move strategy – hence he can handle his ideas in which ever form best suits them, unhampered by any restrictions or constructive fetters. Add to this that he is gifted with a delicate, spontaneous artistic touch, combined with untiring patience in polishing his problems, and the reader will more easily realise how, at the age of 35, though active in the engrossing profession of law, he is already the winner of over 70 tourney honours, including 25 first prizes.

Mr Heathcote continued to take part in national and international tourneys and won at least fifty first prizes. He was known as 'the Manchester problemist' and 'the prince of four-move composers'. The last newspaper mention I found was when the 'famous veteran' was awarded '1st Prize in the British Chess Federation's Composing Tourneys, 1930-40'.[1] He must still have been active while he was living at the Savoy, for he was president of the British Chess Problem Society from 1951 to 1952, the year of his death.

Mr Heathcote, the Prince of Chess. Portrait by Frederick Orrett (1858-1939). (From Chess Notes by Edward Winter)

1   *Falkirk Herald*, 24 July 1940.

He left the stately sum of nearly £37,000 to his wife and son. Mrs Heathcote continued to live at the Savoy until about 1958 when she moved to live with her son in Hornby. She died in a nearby nursing home in 1963.

The Lady with the Cat

ALTHOUGH MRS ALBINO only lived at the Savoy for two or three years, from 1949 to 1951, we children knew her fairly well, partly because of her cat, Marvel.

She lived in a room with a private bathroom on the ground floor of the new wing. When we were playing outside in the garden we'd sometimes see her standing at the top of the stairs at the back door calling 'Marvel, Marvel!' in her quavering voice. We'd immediately add our loud voices to hers and start searching. Usually her pale ginger cat suddenly appeared out of the bushes. It wore a tinkly bell around its neck, but that didn't help much as Mrs Albino didn't seem to hear it.

She often interrupted our games by calling for us to come and help her: we had to hold her arm, or let her support herself on our shoulder, as she descended the steps into the garden. We found this rather annoying, and Nicholas, who was about four or five at the time, once told her what he thought:

'Why do you still go out?' he said. 'You're much too old!'

'Really, do you think so?'

'Yes. Old people should stay in bed.'

'Indeed, perhaps you're right,' Mrs Albino laughed.

Mrs Albino was not predestined to become a rich lady, as neither she nor her husband was born into the upper classes. Mrs Albino's father, John Hurlbutt, had been a farmer, but in the 1871 census he was an innkeeper at the Hind Hotel in Leicester. Ten years later, his daughter (Mary Jane Ann, the future Mrs Albino), then aged sixteen, was at a boarding school in Ipswich, while her future husband, Henry Charles Albino, was working as an assistant to his widowed mother, a licensed victualler (i.e. innkeeper) in Leicester. (According to the 1851 census the latter had been a straw bonnet hatmaker in Bourton-on-the-Water, where her Italian-born husband had been a jeweller.)

The couple married in Leicester in 1886. In the 1891 census, they were living in Edmonton, Middlesex, and Mr Albino's profession was shipbroker's clerk; they had a one-year-old son, and employed a seventeen-year-old domestic servant. By the 1911 census, they were living in Streatham, London, and had three sons. Now Mr Albino was registered as a merchant, and they had a cook and a housemaid. In 1921 the Albinos – presumably after Mr Albino's retirement – were living in Bourton-on-the-Water at the Manor House, a 1919 Cotswold style reconstruction with stone from a demolished manor.[1]

Mr Albino died in 1925, leaving over £42,000 to his wife and children. The youngest son died in 1928 at the age of twenty. In 1935 Mrs Albino and her eldest son embarked from Southampton on a trip to Tangier, travelling first class. Mrs Albino continued to live at the Manor House until about 1949 when she was registered as living at the Savoy. She died in 1954 at the age of eighty-eight. Her eldest son, Harry Hurlbutt Albino (1889–1957), continued to live in the Cotswolds. He was a locally well-known artist, photographer and folk song collector and composer.[2]

The Clergyman's Daughter and her Brother

I CAN STILL PICTURE Miss Urling Smith: she was a small lady with sparse grey hair tied up in a tight bun at the back of her neck. I remember her brother too: he was tall with a nice head of white hair. I later found out that their father had been an Anglican clergyman. In her youth, Emily Laura Urling Smith seems to have been interested in architecture, for in 1898, when she was twenty-four, she passed, with distinction, an Oxford Extension Examination in architecture.[3] However, while her brother Frederick enjoyed a career as a colonial civil servant in West Africa, she stayed at home with her parents until their deaths. Afterwards she continued to live in Prestbury, where her father had had his last appointment. She was joined by her brother after his retirement at about the age of fifty, and in the *1939 England and Wales Register* the household comprised four persons: Mr Urling Smith and his sister (who gave her occupation as 'unpaid domestic duties'), an elderly female domestic worker, and a retired tea planter of the same age as Mr Urling Smith. The Urling Smiths moved to the Savoy in about 1951, where they occupied two small rooms on the third floor.

One day, when I was about ten, I happened to be with Miss Urling Smith up in her room – I'm not quite sure why. She showed me the fine view from her window. You could see several church steeples, and somehow I found myself explaining to her what I had learned at my convent school: that there was only one true church and that was the Holy Roman Catholic one. The more she, the daughter of an Anglican clergyman, protested, the more I insisted. This did not please her, and she later told my father about our

1   https://britishlistedbuildings.co.uk/101341630-manor-house-bourton-on-the-water
2   https://www.efdss.org/learning/resources/beginners-guides/35-english-folk-collectors/2429-efdss-harry-albino
3   *Cheltenham Chronicle*, 22 January 1898.

Aerial view of Cheltenham, 1937. The church on the left is the Roman Catholic one.
(From Robert Beacham, Cheltenham as it was… a pictorial presentatiom, Hendon
Publishing Co Ltd, 1976)

conversation. He was quite cross with me for having quarrelled with a guest, and insisted that I go and apologise.

At school we regularly sang a hymn to St Agnes in which we prayed to be 'ready our blood to shed, / forth as the martyrs led / the path of pain to tread / and die like thee'. Yet my attempts at sainthood had been in vain and I had to obey my father. Heavy-hearted and fearsome, I trod my path of pain, step by step up to the third floor, and knocked at the door. A crumpled little woman with long straggly grey hair hanging about her shoulders opened the door.

'Oh, it's you, Helen. Come in. I was just brushing my hair.'

'Daddy said I had to apologise,' I stuttered unconvincingly.

'Ah, yes, I did talk to him. You see…'

I don't remember what she said, no doubt something about all Christians worshipping the same God. However, I do remember feeling rather sorry for her because, besides not having the gift of the True Faith, she was so pitifully old and ugly.

She offered me a sweet before releasing me.

On one occasion Miss Urling Smith also shocked – or amused – my mother. It must have been in 1962 when she and her brother had moved to rooms on the ground floor of a smaller hotel just nearby. My mother knew the proprietress, Mrs Miklasz, so she will have had the information from her.

Apparently Mr Urling Smith was very poorly and thought to be approaching death. Because he was very tall, his sister, who wanted to be prepared for the event, was worried that any available coffins might turn out to be too short. But she didn't know exactly how tall her brother was. So, before the poor man was taken to a nursing home, she rang up the undertakers and asked them to come and measure him. The undertakers deemed the idea unseemly and refused. Mr Urling Smith died in May 1962 at the age of ninety-one – no doubt he was buried in a suitable coffin. His sister died in Banbury, Oxfordshire, in 1967. She was ninety-three.

The Colonial Colonel and his Artistic Wife

WHEN THE URLING SMITHS left the Savoy (about 1957) their rooms were taken by Colonel and Mrs Vickers.

Mrs Vickers, née Hilda Louise Elmslie, was born in London in 1874, the daughter of an architect. In 1901 she was living with her widowed mother and two domestic servants in Lansdown Crescent, Cheltenham. According to the same census the family of her future husband (his parents, two unmarried sisters, a cook, a housemaid and a Swiss manservant) were then living just nearby, in Lansdown Terrace. So Colonel and Mrs Vickers probably first met in Cheltenham, which is where they married in 1907.

Colonel Aubrey Vickers was born in 1878, the youngest of eight children. Like his father and two of his brothers, he had a military career. He served in the Indian Army, so until his retirement in 1934 his country of

Lansdown Crescent. (Bryan Little, Cheltenham in Pictures, David & Charles, 1967)

Lansdown Terrace. (Bryan Little, Cheltenham in Pictures, David & Charles, 1967)

permanent residence was India. Subsequently he and his wife (who had been with him in India) lived in Essex where Aubrey ran a farm of 153 acres and Mrs Vickers painted. She was a painter in oils and a member of the Ipswich Art Club from 1936 to 1939 exhibiting pictures locally with titles like 'Still Life', 'Midhurst', 'Essex Harvest' and 'The Pool in the Wood'. A painting of a West Angami Naga in full dress is in the collection of the Centre of South Asian Studies, University of Cambridge.[1] Later, the couple lived in Devon, before coming to the Savoy in 1957, where they stayed until 1962.

Colonel Vickers was quite a character. He had a 'gammy leg' that didn't bend, so climbing the stairs to his room on the third floor was quite an ordeal. However, he battled on with soldierly fortitude, counting the steps as he mounted, or – if things grew really bad – mounting to the rhythm of *The Grand Old Duke of York* that he chanted loudly enough to be heard in the reception office:

The grand old Duke of York, *(clompety clomp)*
He had ten thousand men; *(clompety clomp)*
He marched them up to the top of the hill, *(clompety clomp)*

1   https://suffolkartists.co.uk/index.cgi?choice=painter&pid=1725

And he marched them down again. *(clomp clomp. Pause as he reached the half landing.)*

Colonel Vickers had gentlemanly manners. He'd hold the door open for his wife to enter the dining room before him. When she reached their table he'd step behind her and pull out her chair, bringing it back under her knees as she sat down. Then he'd go round to his side, pull out his chair far enough for him to get his stiff leg under the table, drop down so heavily into the chair that we feared it might collapse under his weight; and then, letting his stick fall to the floor, he'd stretch out both arms and pull the table towards him, causing his wife to correspond by jiggling her chair back into position. As soon as both were settled in their places, Colonel Vickers would pick up his table-knife and tap his glass for service.

As Colonel and Mrs Vickers had spent many years in India – he often talked about trout fishing in Kashmir and holidays in Simla – dreary English winters were not something they appreciated. So they regularly moved to Madeira for the winter months. There they stayed at the exclusive Reid's Palace Hotel whose famous guests over the years included, among many others, Albert Schweizer, George Bernard Shaw, Charlie Chaplin and Winston Churchill.

The couple left the Savoy in 1962 and spent the last years of their lives in Lyme Regis, the 'Pearl of Dorset'. Colonel Vickers died there in 1967 aged eighty-nine; his wife died two years later at the age of ninety-five.

The Spiritualist

Although Mrs Frances A Ludolf only lived at the Savoy for about two years, we children knew her well. She was a severe woman of majestic proportions, and the only guest we disliked – a feeling she probably reciprocated.

The problem was that her room was directly above ours. Although we always tried to be quiet, we couldn't help disturbing her: six small children in the room beneath yours cannot be inaudible. That was bad enough, but worst of all for Mrs Ludolf was the fact that Tony had started piano lessons and had to practise for half an hour every day. Not only did this disturb Mrs Ludolf, it also disturbed her deceased husband's spirit so that he refused to appear. At least, that's what Mrs Ludolf told my parents, and her being a spiritualist was another reason for our suspicion and mockery.

Of course, Mrs Ludolf might have been a perfectly nice woman, but she probably wasn't used to children – she'd had none of her own. So, when she talked to us and thought she was giving us good advice, we considered that she

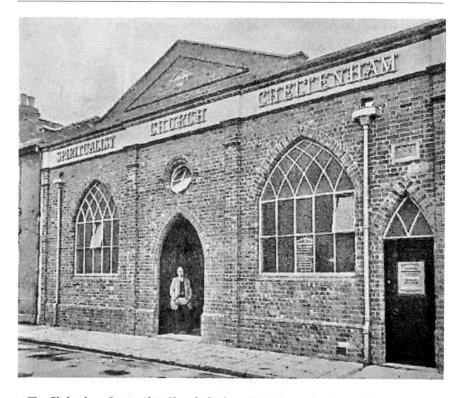

The Cheltenham Spiritualist Church, built in 1926–27 on land specially purchased by Henry Bubb, the uncle of Miss Olive Bubb who resided at the Savoy during the 1950s.

was being bossy. One day in the garden, when I was playing with our tortoise, she told me that it wouldn't be able to get back into its box on its own. She was right, but I answered cheekily, 'It got out by itself, so it must be able to get back in.' I worried for days afterwards that she'd tell my father and that I'd have to apologise. But nothing happened.

Things might have improved for Mrs Ludolf in 1952, after we'd moved into our new house in the hotel garden. But then building began on the conversion of our former rooms into a bar and a grill room. That must have been the last straw. Mrs Ludolf soon moved to Douro Lodge, a private residential hotel in nearby Lansdown Crescent, that might have been recommended to her by other guests, the Misses Brightwell, who had lived there before coming to the Savoy. She died there in 1969, leaving behind quite a fortune: over £60,000 (equivalent to over a million today[1]).

All that I could find out about Mrs Ludolf, who was already a widow when we knew her, is that she was born in Leeds in 1880. Her husband,

1   https://www.officialdata.org

George Herman Ludolf, who was also born in Leeds (in 1875), was the son of a flax merchant and became a merchant himself. By 1910 he was engaged in the Egyptian Civil Service, and in 1921 he was awarded the Order of the Nile (Fifth Class) from the Sultan of Egypt. Afterwards he seems to have been in Batavia, Indonesia, whence he returned in 1928 together with his wife. By then he had retired. Later, the couple lived in the Channel Islands, at least until 1938. Mr Ludolf died in 1946 on the Isle of Man, leaving all his effects (£22,661 19s) to his wife.

The Silk Merchant's Daughters

BY THE TIME they came to the Savoy, Florence and Helen Brightwell were already in their late seventies and Florence was hard of hearing. She had a hearing aid that she held in her hand and thrust towards whoever was talking to her – like a reporter doing an interview.

The two sisters were from Southend-on-Sea where their father had been a silk mercer. They lived there with their parents and three domestic servants in an 18th-century terraced house in Royal Terrace, the promenade overlooking the sea. By 1949 the sisters had moved to Cheltenham and were living at Douro Lodge in Lansdown Crescent.

They moved to the Savoy in 1952. Florence died in 1961 at the age of eighty-seven. Her sister continued to live at the Savoy until her own death in 1966 at the age of ninety-one.

Our Friend in the Garden

MR RHODES (1903–1957) never lived at the Savoy, but his mother lived there from 1946 to 1953, and often had her son brought along to sit in the garden. We used to like talking to him.

We saw him for the first time one day while we were playing in the garden. There he sat, all crumpled up in his wheelchair, his head seeming too big, his face bony, the skin wrinkled, his mouth generous, his eyes lively. Mrs Rhodes, whom we didn't really know but recognised as a guest, introduced him to us.

'This is my son, Mr Rhodes. He's come to sit in the garden and enjoy the sunshine. I have to go away for a moment. Will you keep him company? He likes children.'

'Yes, Madam,' we answered, rather intrigued.

As soon as Mrs Rhodes had disappeared, we interrogated her son.

'Can't you walk at all?' Nicholas asked.

'No, I'm afraid not.' He had a deep crackly voice.

'But could you walk when you were younger?'

'No. I was born like this.'

'Oh! But why?'

'Well, you see, I had a twin brother. We were joined up.'

I'd read about the Siamese twins Chang and Eng in the *Reader's Digest*. They were joined near their ribs. Mr Rhodes didn't look at all like them.

'Oh, I know. Siamese twins! But where's your brother?'

'He died when we were born.'

'Oh, that's awful! But you were a baby, so you didn't notice.'

'Of course not. I never knew him. But I'm still sorry that I haven't got a brother.'

'Haven't you got any brothers and sisters?' Tony asked, knowing how important it was to have brothers and sisters.

'Unfortunately not,' he replied. He seemed really sad, so I changed the subject.

'Where were you and your brother joined?' I asked.

'Here.' He leaned forward and showed us what looked like a pincushion attached to the nape of his neck.

'But that looks like a pincushion,' said Heidi.

'No, it isn't a pincushion, just a bit of padding, so that the place doesn't get sore when I lean back.'

Once all that had been settled, Mr Rhodes became a friend. He quite often came to the garden. We chatted, he watched us play, and sometimes he asked us to pick up something he'd dropped, or to move his wheelchair into the shade or into the sunshine. As far as I remember he also gave Tony some old books, one being an 1887 edition of *Little Lord Fauntleroy*, the traditional story of a poor but highly intelligent, good-looking and kind little American boy who turns out to be the son of an English noble. I enjoyed reading it, although I didn't understand the second part where a fearfully vulgar woman appears and claims, without success of course, that it is her son who is the rightful heir.

The Gentleman who bought Racehorses

M<small>R</small> H<small>OWARD</small> only lived at the Savoy for a couple of years at the beginning of the fifties, but we noticed him because he always wore riding breeches, even in the dining room. We imagined that this was because he did a lot of riding; and we had a theory that his close affinity to horses had affected his physiognomy, for his face was long and flattened like that of a horse. We secretly called him 'Horseface'.

We didn't know that he had been a racehorse owner and that he had twice won the Grand National: in 1907, with Eremon, a former carthorse that he'd bought for fifty pounds; and in 1910, with a horse named Jenkinstown.[1]

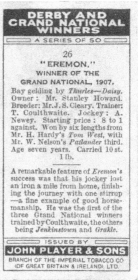

Player's cigarette card recto and verso showing Eremon, the winner of the Grand National 1907.

Clearly, to be the owner of racehorses presupposes a certain financial background.

Stanley MacKnight Howard, born in 1872, was the eldest child of a wrought iron tube manufacturer. He grew up in an early eighteenth-century mansion in Stone, Worcestershire, went to Eton College and then to Oxford University. At that time, according to the 1891 census, his father was a JP, county councillor, and director of Lloyd & Lloyd, one of the largest iron and steel tube manufacturers in England. The household, with five children, employed a housekeeper, a nurse, a parlourmaid, a housemaid, a kitchenmaid, a valet and a coachman/groom.

It is not clear exactly what profession Mr Howard followed after his graduation, but he seems to have worked in his father's business.[2] In 1911, aged thirty-nine, he married Dorothea E McFarland, a distant relative from Ireland, seven years his senior. After living for some years at a farm in Bishop's Cleeve (conveniently near Cheltenham Racecourse), the couple moved to a house in the town.

1   www.horseracinghistory.co.uk; https://www.bonhams.com/auctions/21325/lot/654/

2   In the *1939 England and Wales Register* he is listed as a retired iron tube manufacturer.

STANLEY MACKNIGHT HOWARD = DOROTHEA ELIZABETH
McFARLAND.

STANLEY MACKNIGHT HOWARD, born in Worcestershire on 14th February, 1872.
Educated at Eton and New College, Oxford. Married at St. Margaret's,
Westminster, on 27th February, 1911, Dorothea Elizabeth McFarland,
daughter of James McFarland, of Seapoint, Rostrevor, Ireland, and his
wife Dora Thompson. She was born at Newry on

Address : Seapoint, Rostrevor, Co. Down, Ireland.

Announcement of the marriage of Stanley McKnight Howard and Dorothea Elizabeth McFarland.

In 1949 they came to the Savoy. After Mrs Howard's death the following year, her husband left the Savoy, but he was back again from 1951 to 1952. He died at a Cheltenham nursing home in 1956.

Two Spinster Sisters

THE TWO MISS JONES, Mary Helena and Gertrude Emily, were very tiny, very old ladies whose table in the dining room was just inside the entrance. They always made sure to be in their seats before the other guests arrived. As the first people came in, the elder Miss Jones, whose eyesight was very weak, would pick up a pair of binoculars that seemed too large for her wrinkly little hands. She'd scrutinise each guest and greet those she recognised. However, she was more interested in the guests she didn't recognise.

'Who's that, my dear?' she'd whisper rather loudly because her sister was hard of hearing.

'We don't know him. I don't think he's been here before.'

'A nice-looking young man! I wonder if he's here on business.'

'He might easily be. He's certainly smartly dressed.'

This always amused us, but was rather disconcerting for certain guests: few people enjoy running the gauntlet.

The ladies seem to have lived uneventful lives. Their father had been the vicar of Westbury-on-Severn and, at the same time, rural dean of the Forest of Dean. After his death in 1898 the two sisters, who were now in their thirties, continued to live with their mother (and two domestic servants). Their mother died in 1921, and the two ladies moved to Cheltenham where they occupied a fine house in St Stephens Road.

They moved to the Savoy Hotel in 1948. There they stayed for seven years, before returning to St Stephens Road – not to their old house, but to the Bayshill Nursing Home which is where they both died: Gertrude Emily in 1955 at the age of ninety-one, and Mary Helena in 1958 at the age of ninety-five.

The Lady without Skills

Miss Bubb was already eighty-two in 1953 when she came to live at the Savoy. She occupied a room with a private bathroom. She was a convert to Catholicism and sometimes exchanged Catholic books with my mother.

I remember going to her room to return a book, and then staying on for a chat. I made her a cup of tea while I was there. She was full of admiration.

'How clever young girls are today!' she said. 'I never learned to do anything. I don't know how to make a cup of tea. I can't even dress myself without help: I've never dressed myself alone in all my life!'

Indeed, a woman came in twice a day to help her, but as Miss Bubb was so old, no one thought anything of it. Of course, she might have been exaggerating.

Miss Bubb was particularly fond of my youngest sister, Susy, to whom she liked to offer grubby sweets that she dug out from huge handbags. One day she even gave her a gold bracelet.

Born into an old established Gloucestershire family in 1871, Miss Olive Bubb came from a very wealthy family. Her paternal grandfather owned a 180-acre farm employing ten labourers in Badgeworth near Cheltenham. Her father went into the wool business and became the manager of Bonds Woollen Cloth Mills in Stonehouse, near Stroud. This is where Olive, the eldest of six children, grew up.

By 1901, Miss Bubb, then twenty-nine, was living independently on the Ullenwood estate in Coberley near Cheltenham. She had a housekeeper, a cook, two housemaids and a parlourmaid. The estate (985 acres) and its manor

Bonds Mill in the 1920s. Miss Bubb's father was the manager in the 1870s and 1880s.

Ullenwood manor owned by Miss Bubb's uncle, who also owned the 985-acre estate.
(National Star Foundation)

were owned by her uncle Henry, a leading member of the Spiritualist church in Cheltenham, and his wife Sarah.[1]

In the 1911 census Miss Bubb was registered as a lodger with private means at Wesley House, Bisley, Stroud. It is not clear whether this was her permanent address. Anyway, by 1939 she was living in Cheltenham, sharing accommodation with her spinster cousin, Evelyn M. Bubb.[2] The latter and her brother had together inherited over £200,000 (worth about £14 million today) from the sale in lots of Ullenwood manor and estate after their father's death in 1931.[3] Nevertheless, the two Miss Bubbs lived relatively modestly with only four domestic servants: a housekeeper, a handyman, a housemaid and a cook.

A couple of years after her cousin's death in 1947, Miss Bubb moved to the Savoy where she died ten years later, in 1957. In a short article entitled 'Bequests to Churches', the *Birmingham Post & Gazette* informed the public that Miss Olive Margaret Bubb left '£12,564 (£11,154 net)', of which she bequeathed £100 to each of the Catholic churches in Cheltenham and Gloucester, and smaller sums between £25 and £50 to two clergymen in Cheltenham and Gloucester, her nurse, her chambermaid, and also to my parents.

This is the only mention of Miss Bubb that I found in the papers. She must have led an altogether quieter life than her contemporary, Miss Peatfield.

1   https://www.british-history.ac.uk/vch/glos/vol7/pp174-183 - p16
2   *1939 England and Wales Register.*
3   *England & Wales, National Probate Calendar (Index of Wills and Administrations), 1858-1995* (1931 - Aaron-Cyzer).

8
The Hotel Staff

The Housekeeper and the Assistant Manageress

THE TWO STAFF MEMBERS we children knew best were Miss Elliott, the hotel housekeeper, and Miss Thurston, the assistant manageress. They lived in two rooms on the top floor of the hotel. We were very fond of them and they were fond of each other. They must have known each other for quite some time as they had both worked at the Hotel Majestic in Cheltenham before coming to the Savoy.

Miss Thurston, who came to the Savoy in 1948, was born in 1903. She was an imposing, full-bosomed woman with a cheerful rosy face and black hair tied in a bun. As she spent much of her time in the office that was just opposite our rooms, we saw her several times a day. My brother Nicholas remembers that she always wore a big brown agate broach. I remember her for getting me an autograph from Agatha Christie who was staying at the hotel – I was too shy to ask for it myself.

We were sad and worried when we heard one day that Miss Thurston had breast cancer. She went to the hospital for treatment, but died in 1954.

Miss Elliott was born in 1900. She was from Stroud. She came to the Savoy in 1947 and continued to live and work there until her retirement at the age of sixty-five. An inconspicuous, roundish woman with fine grey-brown hair tied into a tight bun, she was altogether smaller and paler than Miss Thurston.

We loved going and 'helping' her in the food store down in the basement. There she portioned out the provisions needed by the chambermaids: tea (in leaves, not bags), sugar and milk for early morning teas, little bars of soap for the guest rooms, soda and soap flakes for cleaning and washing-up. The soap flakes always made us sneeze. I think she also had bread, butter, eggs and bacon for the breakfast cook. Perhaps also smoked haddock and kippers! We'd sit on the stepladder that she used to reach the upper shelves, and sometimes she gave us a lump of sugar or some raisins. She was a good listener, and my sister Heidi remembers how, at a later date when she was unhappily working in the office, Miss Elliott found the right words to cheer her up.

Boots in 1960.

Miss Elliott was a reader. She was a member of Boots Booklovers Library. Sometimes she asked me to return a book for her and get a new one. She said the librarian knew what books she liked – doctor-nurse romances.

I was about twelve when we bought our first gramophone. When we told Miss Elliott, she gave us her collection of 78 rpm records. It consisted mainly of songs that must have been popular in the twenties and thirties. So the first crackly records we heard over and over again and that I still remember were John McCormack singing *The Trumpeter* and *Danny Boy*, Al Jolson with *I'm Sitting On Top of The World*, Caruso with Gounod's *Ave Maria*; and my favourite, *Lo, Here the Gentle Lark*, sung by the marvellous coloratura singer Amelita Galli-Curci accompanied by the flautist Manuel Berenguer. We'd try, not very successfully, to sing along with her. It was so beautiful. The song still comes into my mind whenever I'm in the countryside and hear the song of larks.

Sometimes we wondered why neither Miss Thurston nor Miss Elliott ever married, as they were so nice and also liked children. Our parents told us it was

Label on one of the gramophone records given to us by Miss Elliott.

because so many young men had been killed in the First World War that there weren't enough bachelors to go round.

Our Faithful Dishwasher and her Assistant

Rose E A Sowray worked at the Savoy as a dishwasher from 1945 until at least 1958.

We knew Rosie well because, from an early age, we sometimes had to help her. She was no longer a very young woman – perhaps thirty, perhaps forty. The first time I remember helping her, the equipment in the stillroom was old-fashioned to say the least. The washing-up was done by hand in a large double-well teak sink. It was too deep for us children, so we only did the drying-up while Rosie washed. Of course we chatted, but we found Rosie rather wearisome as she had a tendency to say the same things over and over again. But we didn't say anything because we knew that she was 'simple-minded' and that she signed for her wages with an X. Later someone taught her to write ROSIE.

Working conditions improved when a dishwasher was installed. You filled a tray with the dirty dishes and cutlery and pushed it into the machine from the left. As soon as the machine had finished working, you slid the tray with the clean dishes out to the right and pushed in a new load of dirty dishes from the left. As it was easy for several people to work without getting into each other's way, we occasionally helped Rosie. The old residents considered it polite to leave some food on their plates to show they had had enough, so one child scraped it off into a bucket for the pig farmer who came by every day. A second child stacked the tray, while Rosie took away the clean and already dry dishes and cutlery and placed them in the cupboards where they belonged.

For most of the time that Rosie worked at the Savoy she lived in one of the small rooms above the stillroom. She had a sister who came regularly and looked after her. Also, my mother used to go up to her room from time to time to make sure that she kept it in order, that she had clean clothes and that she was happy.

When we moved to the house in the garden, there were still many rats and mice around from the stables that had once stood there. So we acquired a cat. He was called Toby and really did catch rats as well as mice. He was a favourite of Rosie's. Every day we could go and collect a bowl of food she'd lovingly put together from the guests' leftovers. Before handing it over, she'd point out what delicacies she'd found. And indeed Toby flourished and would have scorned tinned food.

Sometimes Rosie was helped by a white-haired gentleman named John. I say 'gentleman' because in age and genteel behaviour he was like any of the residents. He had a trembly voice and seemed much too old to be still working. Usually there was a drop hanging precariously from his aristocratic nose. He only worked part-time, his main job being cleaning the silver – particularly teaspoons and forks that turned yellow from the breakfast eggs.

The Linen Keeper

Mrs Curtis was the linen keeper. I loved going downstairs to help her, and Heidi often came too. Mrs Curtis worked in two rooms directly beneath ours. The room you came into from the corridor was the bigger of the two and contained the large airing cupboards with all the linen.[1] There was a fireplace with a radiant fire gas heater, the same as in all the guest rooms; on the mantelpiece there was a heavy black iron figurine of St George killing the dragon. A door led to a smaller room that contained Mrs Curtis's sewing machine and an ironing table.

Mrs Curtis didn't have any children. She lived in a caravan with her husband and a greyhound. She told us that the dog had a proper bed with sheets and a blanket.

Every day, she received the 'departures list' from the office, so that she knew exactly what linen she had to get ready for the chambermaids to collect first thing in the morning. Later, when they brought down their big piles of dirty linen, we could make ourselves useful. We counted the pillowcases and Mrs Curtis filled in the numbers on the list for Crooke's Laundry. When that

---

1   Already in 1925-26 the Hotel Curtis brochure boasted that 'a much-appreciated service is provided for guests by the linen-airing hot-cupboard'.

was done, we helped her count the single sheets and the double sheets – there were no fitted sheets in those days. Then the face towels, the hand towels and the bath towels. There were also tablecloths, serviettes and tea towels from the dining room that had to be counted. Everything was roughly folded and placed in big wicker laundry baskets together with the relevant lists. We closed the baskets using the leather straps that were attached.

Hotel laundry basket.

Crooke's came every day around midday to collect the baskets of dirty washing and deliver the clean linen. So, every afternoon one of Mrs Curtis's jobs was to check the delivery to make sure that nothing was missing. At the same time she examined each piece for stains or tears. We sometimes gave her a hand with the sheets, holding the ends and then helping her fold them up again before she piled them neatly in the cupboards. If there was a tear or a hole Mrs Curtis mended it on the sewing machine. And if new linen had been bought, she changed the thread in the machine to red and wrote 'Savoy Hotel' in joined-up writing in a corner of each piece. I enjoyed watching her do this.

Presumably, Mrs Curtis also received bags of laundry from the guests, but we never had anything to do with that, though we did help our mother fill in the lists of our own dirty washing that also went to Crooke's.

Mrs Curtis had one oddity. Shortly after a telephone extension had been installed in the linen room Tony happened to be present when the phone rang. Mrs Curtis shrank back.

'Aren't you going to pick up the phone?' Tony asked.

'Goodness no!' she replied trembling slightly. 'Such a newfangled contraption! I never asked to have it, did I? I've no idea how to use it. No, no, you can answer if you want!'

I don't know whether or not Mrs Curtis ever surmounted her fear of telephones.

Receptionists

M ISS PHYLLIS MARION WHEELER, the daughter of a commercial clerk
from Bristol, was already working as a receptionist at the Savoy when
we arrived in 1945. She was then aged forty-two, and I remember her as a
slight, dark-haired, quietly busy lady. We children liked her. She worked – and
lived – at the Savoy until 1957.

She was replaced by Miss Chapman who worked as my father's assistant
manageress. She was a friendly lady and good with the guests. However, she
frequently abandoned her 'hotel smile' and looked miserable, which is why we
secretly called her Happy Chappy. She'd purse her lips as though in pain, and
when we asked what was the matter, she'd grimace saying, 'Nothing, it's just
my stomach'. Apparently she suffered from heartburn. It turned out that she
had a stomach ulcer. She must have recovered, because some years later she
moved on to become the manageress of the Lilley Brook, a fine hotel adjoining
the Cheltenham golf course on Cleeve Hill.

Before the time of computers and email, credit cards, smart phones,
internet and social media, a hotel receptionist's duties were more complicated
than they are today. Things had not changed much by 1964, when I helped out
for several months.

Here is a chronological list of a receptionist's tasks at the Savoy in those
days.

Departures: if necessary, ring for the porter and tell him which room to
fetch the luggage from. Finalise the bill and receive payment by cheque or in
cash. Perhaps, order a taxi.

Sort the post and place letters for guests into their pigeonholes.

Answer letters – back then, many reservations were made by post. There
were also enquiries about terms for extended stays. Letters were typed on a
manual typewriter on hotel stationery and with a carbon copy.

Type the menus for luncheon and dinner onto wax stencils. Then print
out the required number using the
Roneo machine. (Photocopiers were
not yet on the market.)

All the while you had to take
incoming phone calls. Sometimes
you answered them yourself, taking
reservations for rooms or for tables in
the restaurant or giving information.
But a call might be for the manageress
or someone at the end of one of the

*Copying machine similar to the one we used
in the 1950s. (eracommons.ca)*

few extensions. If that was the case, you had to push down the relevant switch on the switchboard and turn a handle for the bell to ring.

The afternoons continued in much the same way, except that instead of departures you now had arrivals. The new guests filled in their names and addresses in the guest book and were asked if they wanted afternoon tea or dinner, if they wished for a call or early morning tea the next

Switchboard similar to the one we had in the reception office. (icollector.com)

morning, and what newspaper they would like to order. Then they were taken to their rooms by the porter, while the receptionist recorded their bookings for the information of the dining room and the chambermaids.

In between the various interruptions, the receptionist had to keep the daily ledger up to date. For obvious reasons, we called it the sheet. It had all the residents' names and room numbers down the left hand side, and about a dozen columns spread out from there to the right with headings for different charges. These charges were added up for each resident and entered into the 'totals' column on the right hand side of the sheet. Then each column was added up from top to bottom. Finally, the totals at the foot of each column were tallied, resulting, if you were lucky, in a sum identical to the one already in the bottom right hand corner of the sheet. Eventually I became quite proficient at adding up pounds, shillings and pence. But in the beginning, it often happened that the totals refused to tally so that I had to ask my father to come and find my mistake, otherwise I'd have been in the office all night! Later we had a little adding-up machine.

Waiters and Waitresses

IN ABOUT 1948, when I was seven and a half and Heidi nearly six, we changed from St Gregory's School to Charlton Park Convent School in Charlton Kings. We were too young to go to school by bicycle, so we used to take the bus that left at twenty past eight from the stop at the bottom of Bayshill Road. As a result, we had to have our breakfast earlier than the other guests, who weren't served until eight o'clock. We were attended by whosoever was on duty at the time. This meant that we had many conversations with waiters and waitresses that we couldn't have had if there had been guests waiting to be served – or indeed if our parents had been present.

John Ivanovitch was our headwaiter. He was Russian, or perhaps Ukrainian, and had a lovely foreign accent. He was a proper waiter, very well-mannered, and always correctly dressed in a black suit, white shirt and black tie. He knew how to fold serviettes into all kinds of shapes, and showed us how to make a boat, a fan, a bishop's hat and a flower. He also demonstrated how to unpack half a pound of butter and place it on the dish without touching the butter. He often talked about his son who was, by all accounts, a remarkable person – very intelligent, very good-looking and growing fast. In fact he grew so tall – over six foot – that he couldn't fit into an ordinary bed and John had to have one made to measure. We found this all very interesting.

But then John's behaviour changed. He was nervous and easily upset. One day, he complained to my father that he was being persecuted by guests or by other members of the staff. Then he said that people were trying to poison him. No one believed him. He got so worried that he fell ill and had to go to the mental hospital in Gloucester. My mother took me there one day to visit him. We gave him a box of chocolates. He was very polite but the liveliness had gone.

He didn't come back to the hotel, and I don't think I ever saw him again.

Another interesting foreigner was Doris who was Polish. She was a motherly figure, small, old and dumpy, and she had a strong Polish accent. She loved my mother and had a habit of wanting to kiss her hand – to my mother's embarrassment. One day, when for some reason or other we were having our meal in the 'smoking room' next to the dining room and my father wanted to be sure that all the guests had been served before Doris started serving us, she replied, 'Don't vorry Sir, dey're all lapping up deir soup fery nicely.' We thought this was a funny way of putting it!

Geraldine was very different. She'd arrived from Ireland in about 1951 or 1952 to train as a waitress and, like Rosie, occupied a room above the stillroom. She was much younger than Doris or John, but she must have been at least twenty-one years old since she's listed in the Electoral Register. We liked her because she was very pretty and cheerful, and she spoke with an attractive Irish accent. Tony thought she had the ideal figure for a woman, and particularly admired her splendid bust (no doubt formed by the type of conical bra – also called torpedo or bullet bra – that was fashionable in the fifties). I don't know how long Geraldine worked at the Savoy, but in 1961 she got married, in Cheltenham, to a man named David G Wilkinson.[1]

1   England & Wales, Civil Registration Marriage Index, 1916–2005, vol. 7b, p. 548.

Nora was the headwaitress after John. A tall, attractive woman who liked a good laugh, she might have been in her forties. She had varicose veins. On her doctor's orders she drank a glass of Guinness every day ('Guinness is good for you!'). We were familiar with the beer from the amusing advertisements in the 'My goodness – my Guinness' series, so it was exciting to be allowed to take a sip out of Nora's glass. I found it very bitter! Later, after my first year at university, I had to take on Nora's job for several weeks during the summer holidays because she got a 'poison leg'. I don't remember if she was able to come back to the same job or if she had to find something that was easier on the legs.

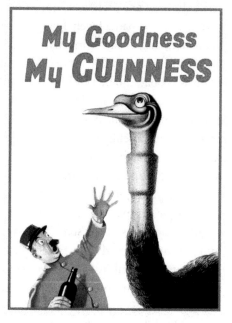

Guinness poster.

Postscript: In May 2021, in reply to a query I posted in the Facebook group 'Days gone by in Cheltenham' I received the following message from a lady called Margaret: 'I came to Cheltenham from the Forest of Dean in 1953 and was employed by your father at the Savoy and lived there for two years. I remember the family very well, such a lovely family.'

I had no memories of Margaret, but I was able to contact her and we had a delightful video chat. Now over eighty years old, Margaret appeared before me as an attractive and lively old lady, still very much with it, happy, and proud of her big family – she'd had five children. She told me that in 1953, at the age of fifteen or sixteen, she came to the Savoy to work as a waitress. She lived in one of the little rooms above the stillroom and was very happy there. The other three rooms were occupied by Rosie and two young girls from Wales who were employed as chambermaids. Apparently the young women got along with one another and had lots of fun. Margaret remembered Geraldine and the headwaiter John and also remembered how pleased she was that, besides her wages, she received 2s 6d a week as her share of the tips..

In 1955 Margaret left the Savoy to get married. She told me that my mother gave her a lovely picture as a wedding present. The family moved to Gloucester and she was kept busy looking after her husband and five children.

Her career as a waitress had been of short duration and she never went out to work again.

Chambermaids

ALTHOUGH I CAN'T REMEMBER the names of many chambermaids, Heidi and I were familiar with their work. When we were in our teens we occasionally 'helped out' for a few days in the school holidays, replacing someone who'd fallen ill or failed to turn up.

You had to start quite early in the morning, in time to prepare and serve early morning tea to those guests who had ordered it. Some guests only wanted a morning call. After that you had your breakfast. Then you began cleaning the rooms, but not the corridors or the public bathrooms and toilets that were cleaned by someone else.

The first thing you had to do was collect the clean linen from the linen room. That sometimes entailed two or three trips up and down stairs – there was no lift at the time. Then you did the rooms, one by one. First you'd have to check if the chamber pot had been used. We were always relieved if it hadn't! If it had, you emptied it into a bucket and rinsed and wiped it. Horrible! Smelly! Then you cleaned the basin, the tooth glass and the mirror. You replaced the soap if there were to be new guests. You emptied the wastepaper basket. After that you made the beds. As you had the departures list, you knew which rooms required fresh bed linen, towels and soap. As for the residents, their towels and pillowcases were changed every week. But of the sheets, only the bottom one was taken away, to be replaced by the top one, that in its turn was replaced by a clean one; then you put on the blanket and the eiderdown and covered the bed with its bedspread. Finally, you did the dusting and hoovered the carpet. You had to be quite quick if you wanted to finish in time for lunch.

Chambermaids also had a short evening shift to 'turn down the beds', i.e. remove the bedspread and fold back the bedcovers so that the guest could get into bed more easily.

I can't remember how many rooms each chambermaid was expected to do, but I think the work was more interesting at the Savoy than in modern hotels: each room was different and differently furnished. And the residents had photographs and nicknacks on their mantelpieces and their own pictures on the walls. There was even one room that had exotic Oriental furniture, probably left there by someone who'd worked and lived in the colonies.

Chambermaids in those days often lived in the hotel, later they had rooms in the house my father bought just opposite the hotel in Royal Parade. They were not well paid, and I suppose that is why they were 'difficult to find' and not always really competent. I remember one day a regular guest complained at the reception that his early morning tea had tasted so horrible that he hadn't been able to drink it. Miss Elliott was informed and subsequently found out that the chambermaid had inadvertently dropped a bar of soap into the kettle and hadn't been able to get it out. She didn't think the guests would notice that the tea had been made with soapy water!

Another chambermaid had a tendency to drink too much of the kind of cider known in the region as 'scrumpy': she once tumbled all the way down the stairs in the staff house, luckily without breaking any bones. And one chambermaid got chased along the new wing corridor by a man (ex-boyfriend?) with a knife. Decidedly, that was not funny, and hardly likely to have been her fault anyway!

There is one chambermaid who was not at all like those three and whom I remember very well, although I was still a small child when I knew her. Her name was Elizabeth. As she was 'our' chambermaid we saw her almost every day and grew fond of her. She was slim and dark-haired, very beautiful in my opinion. She didn't live in the hotel, but somewhere in the neighbourhood. One day, she didn't come to work. The next thing we heard was that she'd died: she'd killed herself by jumping out of a window. We were utterly shocked. How could a clever, grown-up person do something like that? Mummy tried to explain by saying that Elizabeth had been very sad, so sad that she hadn't known what to do, and no one could help her. I pictured Elizabeth standing on a window sill and looking down onto the road far below. How could she have jumped? It was something I couldn't understand.

Porters and Night Porters

P ORTERS AT OUR HOTEL did not need any special qualifications. However, they had a variety of duties, so they had to be versatile.

Their first duty, as the name implies, was portering: they had to carry guests' luggage. They also carried beds, wardrobes, chairs… For example, if a twin-bedded room was let as a single, one of the beds was removed to the new wing cellar. (My brother Tony, who used to lend a hand when he was old enough, said he became expert at getting round tight corners with the huge box-spring mattresses and metal frames – in its brochures, the hotel prided itself on its 'Vi-Spring mattresses in all bedrooms'.)

Besides portering jobs, the porter was responsible for the appearance of the hotel entrance and lobby. He had to do the hoovering and dusting, clean the glass doors and polish the brass handles and handrails. He was also in charge of the gentlemen's toilets. Besides that, he fixed minor technical issues like changing light bulbs. Another rather arduous job, that required some skill, was keeping the coke-fired boilers going, stoking and clinkering them, four in the winter, two in the summer.

The night porter had to bank up the boilers overnight after clinkering, and then make sure the heat was up again in the morning, ready for all the hot water needed for the guests' baths. My brother Tony remembers that, as a boy, he became somewhat of an expert at the 'boiler craft'. After he'd left Cheltenham to go to commercial college in Switzerland, Nicholas took over, and Gabrielle recalls how she helped him take out the clinker. Around 1957 oil heating was installed. Much more convenient, and cleaner too!

In those days people expected their shoes to be cleaned every day. They left them outside their doors, toes out. The night porter picked them up, marking the room number with chalk on the soles. If he was lucky, he might find a sixpence or even a shilling in some shoes. When he'd cleaned them he returned them to their places in front of the doors, toes in. In that way he could see if any had been put out late. The night porter also served drinks after the bar shut, and then tidied the lounge after everyone had left. In the morning he took the newspaper list to the newsagents, collected the papers and delivered them to the rooms. He served any early morning teas that were due before the chambermaids came on duty. It was also his job to give the early morning calls, the method being a hearty bang on the door.

We had a variety of porters and night porters – they seldom stayed for very long. Some had their idiosyncrasies as the following anecdotes show.

One porter I remember was a wiry, rather twitchy middle-aged man. One day my mother, having heard that Princess Margaret would be coming to a small private dinner party, went to the reception to see her arrive. But just as the Princess was coming in through the door, the porter turned up. He was so overwhelmed to find himself in the presence of a member of the Royal Family that he there and then performed a tap dance in her honour. My mother was most embarrassed – it was certainly not the kind of thing you'd expect to see in a first-class hotel!

The second anecdote concerns a night porter. Late one night, when we were already living in our house in the garden, my father was awakened by the alarm going off in the hotel. He quickly dressed and rushed to see what was happening. He found a large number of guests huddled outside the hotel in their dressing-gowns, and the night porter running around and counting them. Many of the guests patted the porter on the back and thanked him for raising the alarm. 'Good fellow! Saved our lives!' The fire brigade arrived and the men raced in with their hoses. They soon found the fire, which caused a lot of smoke but hadn't yet spread. They put it out and the guests could go back to their rooms.

It wasn't until the following morning that my father discovered that the room in which the fire had broken out had been unoccupied. The fire inspector said that it had been intentionally lit. Further investigation revealed that the night porter had previously worked at several hotels in which a fire had broken out. Each time, he had been celebrated as a heroic saviour! He confessed, but he was sacked all the same, as deserved!

The fire did have one positive result: because one guest had slept through all the commotion, the alarm was adjusted so that it could be heard in every single one of the hotel rooms.

Gardeners

OLD WILLIAM, as we called him, was already working for the Savoy when we arrived. I don't suppose he was really old, perhaps still in his fifties. We children were not always on very good terms with him. In fact, after he'd shouted at us a couple of times for damaging his flowers in our ball games, we decided he was our enemy. We had recently founded a secret society that convened in the gap between a hedge and the high wall of the neighbours' garden. Now, at last, we had an agenda: we spent many a happy hour giggling and chatting in our hiding place, working out how best to wreak vengeance on Old William. Fortunately we never proceeded to action, for our plans were shocking: sending him our poo in the post. But the mere plotting had been enough to assuage our thirst for revenge.

Actually, Old William must have been a very good and dedicated gardener. There were flowers in the garden almost all year round: daffodils, crocuses, hyacinths, grape hyacinths and primulas in early spring, followed later by tulips, pansies and sweet-smelling wallflowers. Soon the fruit trees blossomed, and the lilac too. In the summer, besides all the roses on pergolas and bushes, there were delphiniums, snapdragons with mouths you could open and shut, lupins, phlox, peonies, Sweet William and enormous pink and red poppies; fragrant lavender flourished around the pond, along the paths and beneath the rose bushes. Every year the gardener put up long bamboo poles, and gradually the sweet peas climbed up and produced their delicately coloured, sweet-scented blossoms. He put in the dahlia bulbs at the right time, so we had dahlias as autumn approached. There were also asters and Michaelmas daisies. And the tall feathery plumes of maiden grass.

What Old William did not like were daisies and buttercups in the lawn. Sometimes he sprayed weedkiller and they all shrivelled up, leaving brown patches in the grass.

He had a potting shed that smelled of earth. Later we kept a rabbit named Sniffy there, until myxomatosis broke out in the 1950s. We decided that the only way we could stop Sniffy catching the disease and suffering a terrible death was to bring him to the hotel chef for slaughter and cooking. I'm not sure whether we ate the meat. Later my youngest sister Susy kept guinea pigs in the potting shed. She managed to train them as circus animals for family performances.

Mr Lyndon, a more amenable man than Old William, helped him part-time. He was quite old too, tall and so thin he looked fragile.

Old William's successor was Mr Newcombe, who was friendly, hardworking and competent. We children got on with him better than with Old William, as he was very indulgent and had a good sense of humour. He was married, but the couple had no children. Then suddenly, after they'd given up all hope, Mrs Newcombe became pregnant and bore a son. Everyone was delighted. My mother knitted baby clothes, and my father, who strongly believed that a mother's place was in the home and that she certainly shouldn't go out to work, raised Mr Newcombe's salary.

The garden of the Savoy Hotel

9
Later Developments

The New House

WE HAD TO WAIT a long time before we could move out of the hotel and live in a proper house. The dilapidated cottage at the far end of the hotel garden that we wanted to replace was rented to a couple for five shillings a week. It was in a bad state and still had gas lighting. But the couple who were living there did not want to leave, and because of the housing shortage after the war they could not be given notice. However around 1949 the man left his wife. Eventually she, too, moved out of the house.

At last plans could be made and a building permit applied for. My mother's youngest brother, Uncle Moritz, who had recently started his own business as an architect in Lucerne, came to Cheltenham and drew up the plans.

The old cottage at the end of the hotel garden.

Patrick and Michael Flynn, builders, and like my father members of the Catholic organisation the Knights of St Columbus, were contracted to do the building.

It was an interesting time for us, watching the demolition of the old cottage and stables, seeing the great cavity that had been dug out for the cellar, and all the work involved in building a house – our house, the one in which we were going to live! We liked the workers. They often chatted and joked with us, but we were sometimes embarrassed by their Irish accents that we couldn't always understand.

Demolition of the old cottage. Michael Flynn, the man who rescued my sister, is standing fifth from the right, his brother Patrick Flynn second from the right.

Our new house. The edge of the round pond we used to bathe in and from which Gabrielle was rescued can be seen on the left.

One day Mickey Flynn suddenly noticed that there was a child lying in the pond. He fished her out. It was Gabrielle. Unharmed. The pond was only about a foot deep, but that was enough to drown a small child. We were all deeply grateful to Mickey Flynn!

After moving into the new house in 1952 we still continued to have all our meals in the hotel, except for tea that we had *en famille* (but with sandwiches and cakes provided by the hotel) when we got back hungry from school. That was always a joyous meal, except when Daddy was there and insisted on testing Nicholas on his times tables:

'Seven sevens?'

Nicholas surreptitiously tries to work out the sum on his fingers under the table.

'Sixty-three.'

Gabrielle, who's heard the same charade so often, chimes in, 'Forty-nine'.

My father was near despair. He was worried that Nicholas would not pass the 'scholarship', as the '11 plus exam' was called at the time. But he needn't have worried: Nicholas passed and subsequently never had any problems at grammar school.

The Bar and the Grill Room

WHEN MY FATHER bought the hotel it was not licensed to sell alcoholic drinks. In 1946 he was granted a temporary licence 'restricted to residents and guests, and to persons taking meals on the premises', which was later converted into a permanent (but still not a full) licence in 1949.

My father had always been eager to bring the Savoy up to date. I imagine he wanted to get rid of its image as a genteel hotel for wealthy old fuddy-duddies. Now that we had vacated our rooms in the hotel, he could go forward with his plans. My parents' old bedroom was converted into a bar and the adjoining children's living room into a grill room. Our parents' sitting room became a room for private dinner parties and business meetings.

The grill room, where guests could watch the chef cooking their food, was a novelty in Cheltenham. But what was really sensational was that it was open every day of the week, including Sundays when every other restaurant in Cheltenham was closed. It was something Cheltonians had to get used to. So our whole family used to have our Sunday lunch there, sitting at tables by the windows in order to attract customers. It was quite a treat for us, since – unlike during the week – we were allowed to choose what we wanted from the menu. For further promotion, we children composed what we considered to

The bar (formerly our parents' bedroom) with our first barmaid, Fran.

be a poem: 'Why bother to cook / Why worry and fuss / When you could be eating / In comfort with us!'

Whether or not that 'poem' was ever used, the grill room soon became popular, not least thanks to Frank and Bert the chefs and Gerry the waiter, characters who with their homely Gloucestershire accents might have come straight out of *The Archers*. My father did sometimes remonstrate with Bert for serving such large portions of the main course that people couldn't manage a dessert, but I suppose that was one reason for his popularity. Anyway, the main profits always come from drinks, and as Bert was offered so many beers by the clients, this might possibly have made up for any lack of dessert orders. Gerry, too, was good with the clients, and was kept very busy running to and fro. My brother Nicholas remembers how he used to keep a burning fag in the servery for a drag each time he passed by.

My brother-in-law, Robin Pagan, remembers the time the comedian Ronnie Barker came to the grill room. In the course of their conversation he told Robin that the hotel looked much bigger from the outside than it actually was – to which Robin would have answered, had he only thought of it in time: 'Well, that's show business, isn't it!'

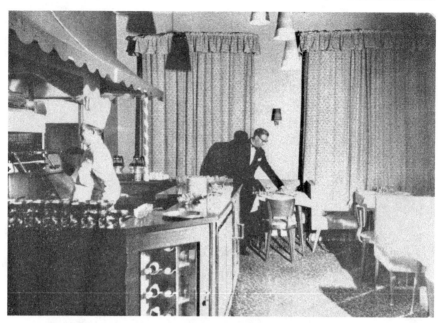

The grill room (formerly the children's room) with Bert and Gerry.

The grill room used plain-coloured Irish linen tablecloths and serviettes. These were not sent to the laundry but washed and ironed by Mrs Malvern at our new house, in the kitchen where we rarely cooked anything. At first she used a single-tub machine and a clothes wringer that fitted over the kitchen sink. Later she had a twin-tub machine with its spin dryer. She ironed using a dry ironing press: a steam press was not necessary, as the laundry was still damp enough. We all knew how it worked because whenever Mrs Malvern couldn't come one of us had to step in. When we came home from school she would often still be at work. We made her a cup of tea that she drank without milk. As a result you always had to scrub her cup to remove the tea stains.

Obviously we got to know Mrs Malvern quite well. She knew that I'd chosen French as one of my A Level subjects, and asked me to help her daughter who was worried about her O Level exam. So I gave her a couple of private lessons... and was relieved when I later heard that she'd passed.

Like the grill room, the bar soon became popular, although at first it was only open to people staying at the hotel or coming for a meal. Indeed, my father had to wait until 1957 to obtain a permit for drinks to be served to all comers.

The grant of a full licence was, for staid Cheltenham, a momentous decision, that could only be reached after a licensing session lasting two and a

OPEN
12—2.30 p.m. and 6—11 p.m.
(12—2 p.m. and 7—10 p.m. Sundays)

MINIMUM
CHARGE
10/6

Savoy Grill

Melon	...	3/-	Grapefruit Cocktail	1/6
Scotch Smoked Salmon	...	8/-	Prawn Cocktail	4/6
Fried Scampi (as Entrée)	...	6/6	Paté Maison	4/-

SOUPS

Clear Turtle Soup	...	4/-	Consommé or Cream du Jour	1/6

OMELETTES (with Fried Potatoes and Peas)
Ham, Mushroom or Cheese ...   7/6

FISH (with Fried Potatoes and Peas)

Fried Scampi, Tartare Sauce	12/6	Dover Sole Grilled	14/-
Fried Fillet of Plaice, Tartare Sauce	8/6	Cold Scotch Salmon	13/6

GRILLS (with Fried Potatoes, Mushroom, Tomato and Peas)

Chateaubriand (two persons)	32/-	Pork Chop	10/-
Fillet Steak	14/-	Lamb Cutlets (two)	9/-
Minute Steak	9/6	Gammon Monte Carlo	9/6
Rump Steak	12/6	Fried Chicken Americaine	10/-
Sirloin Steak	11/-	Cold Chicken Salad	10/-
Mixed Grill	13/6	Cold Turkey Salad	10/-

SWEETS

Pineapple Flambé	8/-	Rum Omelette	7/6
Coupe Jacques	3/-	Peach Melba	3/-
Fruit Salad and Cream	3/-	Ice Cream	1/6

SAVOURIES

Cheese and Biscuits	2/6	Mushrooms on Toast	3/-
Welsh Rarebit	2/6	Sardines on Toast	3/-

Cona Coffee and Cream   ...   2/-
Cona Coffee Black   ...   1/6

A private room is available for sit-down meals for up to 16, or buffet for up to 25 persons.
Restaurant bookings can be accepted, sit-down up to 80, buffet up to 100 persons.
Afternoon Weddings catered for.
Menus on application

A Savoy Grill menu.

half hours![1] For it was 'the first full licence to serve drinks at a residential hotel to be granted in Cheltenham since 1871', bringing the number of such hotels in Cheltenham to eight. The application was strongly opposed by the licensee of a nearby pub who feared the competition and saw 'no evidence of pressing public need for the new licence'. The lawyer representing my father argued that, under my father's management, the Savoy had been converted from a 'rather

1   Information and following quotes from the *Gloucestershire Echo* 1957 (exact date unknown).

dilapidated state' into 'a high-class residential hotel' and added that 'since 1939 no fewer than 21 hotels in Cheltenham had gone out of business. Only one of these had had any kind of licence, and he thought this showed that the trend was now in favour of licensed hotels'. Welcome swinging Cheltenham!

Of course, the award of the full licence boosted trade, the greatest turnovers being achieved during race meetings, especially when someone had had a lucky day – or was even the proprietor of a winning horse.

One regular client of the bar was Godfrey Basely, the inventor of *The Archers*. I remember how he explained that he had to keep a card index of all his characters so as not to get them confused.

Our Second Hotel, the Foley Arms in Malvern

M Y BROTHER TONY had very early been set on the path to become a hotelier. After passing his O Levels he was sent to Lucerne to attend the *Handelsschule,* from which he graduated at the age of eighteen with a commercial diploma. From Lucerne he went on to the Hotel School in Lausanne, and subsequently worked in grand hotels in St Moritz, Zurich, Paris and London, before coming to Cheltenham to assist my father.

The Foley Arms.

This did not work out well – my father was very domineering, and Tony soon became restless and talked about getting a job in London.

But then the Foley Arms, a former coaching inn in Malvern, came on the market. My father asked Tony if he would be interested in taking over the management. He said yes, so my father sold the next-door house that he'd bought some years earlier in case he wanted to extend the hotel, and managed to put together enough money to buy the Foley. This was in 1963.

I become my Father's Assistant

N OW WITHOUT my brother's help my father, who was sixty-five and needed to reduce his work load, began to look around for an assistant. The first person he found turned out to be a competent manageress with a pleasant manner toward both guests and staff. Unfortunately, however, she had an alcohol problem and suddenly quit her job to go for treatment at an alcohol rehab clinic.

Just then I was in temporary employment in a lawyers' office in London, having taken a short secretarial course after my graduation from university. So I could easily give in my notice and step in.

I worked as my father's assistant from September 1964 until the end of the year. Most of the time I was occupied in the reception. The work was interesting and varied and brought some surprises. I particularly remember one stressful evening. Two guests who had just arrived were signing the guest book and I had just rung for the porter to take them to their room when a man came rushing down the stairs and told me there was water coming through the ceiling of his room. At the same time the phone rang and someone wanted to book a room. I think my father came to the rescue and helped get things sorted out.

Sometimes you were interrupted during your work by people who merely wanted to talk, particularly old residents who liked to come to the reception for a chat. I remember one old lady who wanted a taxi to take her to the chiropodist and bored me at length with stories about her toenails. I had to show polite interest but was relieved when the taxi arrived.

One very foggy evening while I was trying to balance the 'sheet', a French client who had dined in the grill room asked me to call for a taxi to take him to his hotel in Worcester. I dialled different companies but no one replied. Finally I heard a grumpy voice at the end of the line.

'Hello!'

'Good evening! Savoy Hotel here. Could you please send a taxi to take a client to Worcester?'

'What? Have you seen the fog? Crazy! To Worcester? You wouldn't get there in ten hours! Good night.' And he hung up.

Cotswold fogs! I remembered how it had taken Tony nearly four hours for the half-hour drive from Cheltenham to Malvern.

'Je suis désolée, Monsieur. Le brouillard est trop épais, les taxis ne roulent pas. Il faut que vous passiez la nuit ici. Voulez-vous que je vous donne une chambre?'

The man had no choice. But he congratulated me on my French!

Once there was a BBC team that had come to Cheltenham for some reason or other and wanted drinks in the lounge after the bar had closed. That would have been the night porter's job, but the man came to me in despair because the guests wanted drinks he wasn't familiar with. So I asked one of them to come to the bar with me and give me instructions, as the only cocktail I knew how to make was a Bloody Mary. I daresay the drinks turned out better than expected, and we had a nice conversation that made me think it would be interesting to work for the BBC. But I had to get back to my 'sheet'.

I regularly had to work in the bar for short periods to relieve the barmaid while she had her meal. It's not something I liked doing. Either you had to try to make conversation with a client, or else you had to pretend not to hear what two clients talking to each other about quite private matters were saying...

Two of my jobs required me to withdraw to a quiet office. The first was preparing for pay day. Most of the staff were paid on a weekly basis. I had to calculate the amounts due (you had to deduct tax and insurance and, for some, add their share of the service charge), then tot everything up and fetch the cash from the bank. After that I'd copy my calculations onto each pay packet, then fill up the packets, remembering not to seal them until I'd finished, the proof that I hadn't made a mistake being that I'd had enough cash and not a penny left over. In the afternoon the people would file into the office and I had the pleasure of handing them their pay.

The other job I did in the quiet office was bookkeeping: paying tradesmen's bills (I now sent the cheques by post instead of taking them by bike!), sending statements to business clients who had an account with the hotel etc.

I think I was reasonably efficient and could have stayed on and learned to run the hotel. But it wasn't what I wanted to do. In the New Year I left for Germany where I started on a career in publishing.

An Enterprising Manager

AN AMBITIOUS YOUNG MANAGER followed. During his time the Savoy was once again modernised and renovated. By 1968 nine bedrooms had received private bathrooms, telephones were installed in all of them and television sets in a few – as an experiment. The most costly parts of the

Tommy Trinder at the Savoy.

modernisation had been the installation of a lift to all floors, and the renovation of the roof over the oldest part of the hotel where there had been trouble with leaks and snow in the winter. The foyer was also modernised, and now included four showcases for the display of objects from local shops.

Besides that, the hotel offered new attractions: an 'intimate' dance floor in the dining room (now always referred to as the 'restaurant') and a 'luxury cocktail bar' adjacent to the restaurant, reserved solely for the use of diners. This was inaugurated on 19 October 1968 with a Saturday Night Dinner and Dance starring the 'famous comedian of stage, screen and television' Tommy Trinder.[1]

1   Advertisement in the *Gloucestershire Echo*, October 1968.

Work on the extension to the new wing.

The manager also had plans for a roof garden where afternoon teas could be served 'among a setting of plants and foliage'.[1] This was never created. The manager felt restricted, my father thought him presumptuous. Soon the manager left for a job where he felt he'd have more scope.

The Second Generation takes over

B ESIDES TONY, Gabrielle was the only one of us who trained for the hotel business. While Tony was managing the hotel in Malvern, she took the three-year Hotel and Catering Course at the Technical College in Cheltenham from 1964 to 1967. After gaining experience at the Mount Royal Hotel in Oxford Street in London for about six months, she returned to work at the Savoy. It was while serving in the bar one evening in September 1968 that she met Robin Pagan. They married the following year and went to live in Durham, where Robin had a post as lecturer in General Studies at the Technical College.

Meanwhile my father was getting older. Something had to change. He asked Robin, who didn't like his work at the college, if he could imagine embarking on a hotel career. Gabrielle already had hotel management training, so with a bit of training himself they would be the ideal couple to take over one of the hotels. Robin decided to give it a try and, in 1970, gave in his notice and came to Cheltenham with his little family. After taking a crash course at the Technical College he started working at the Savoy to learn the ropes, so to speak. During his time there further changes were made to the hotel: two floors with a total of fifteen rooms with ensuite bathrooms were added to the new wing, and on the second floor large double rooms were converted into singles with bathrooms.

In December 1971, Tony and his wife Christine took over the management of the Savoy, while Gabrielle and Robin took over the Foley.

However, only a couple of years later Robin decided to study for the ministry in the United Reformed Church. My father was disappointed but, as he wrote in his memoirs: 'What could I as a Christian say to that but accept!' So in summer 1975 the Pagans left Malvern for Robin to start his training. As Tony didn't want to be the general manager of two hotels, the Foley was eventually sold. Tony continued to run the Savoy, and in 1979 my parents returned to live permanently in Switzerland.

Meanwhile the hotel business was changing rapidly. Cheap flights incited holidaymakers to go abroad; if they stayed in Britain and didn't go to the seaside, they were likely to drive around; and if they happened to come to

1   Quoted from the article that appeared in the *Gloucestershire Echo* in October 1968.

Cheltenham they stayed for no longer than a day or two. With the opening of the M5 southern extension in 1977, journeys were shortened and drivers no longer stopped in Cheltenham for the night; at half-term parents took their children home from boarding school instead of seeing them while staying at a hotel; and chartered accountants and others who went to Cheltenham on business could go home every evening. Some Cheltenham hotels disappeared, transformed into flats or offices; and several of the well-known hotels were taken over by chains.

There was no choice but to adapt. Tony's wife had set up quite a successful beauty salon in the hotel. But to attract clientele more changes were required. That would have involved further investment that neither Tony nor my father was willing to risk.

Besides that, whereas my father had been totally committed to the development of the business that he himself had built up and didn't mind twelve-hour working days, Tony would have preferred a job with fixed hours and fewer responsibilities. He was ready for a change. So as soon as a buyer was found the hotel was sold. This was in 1985.

10
The End of a Dream

MY FATHER had always dreamed of founding a hotel dynasty. For him it was natural that we should help in the hotel from early childhood on and he probably thought that we would automatically want to continue in the field. Although he never put pressure on us to go in for a hotel career, he must have been disappointed that of his six children only two had chosen the profession. Of those two Gabrielle had soon given it up. And now Tony wanted to leave the business! There was nothing he could do, and in the end he and my mother were relieved that the hotel had been successfully sold. They'd settled down very well in Switzerland, where they still had relatives and old friends. They travelled to England very frequently to see their children and their many grandchildren. Later, it was their children and grandchildren who came to Switzerland to see their parents.

After its sale the hotel was renamed several times: from the Savoy it became the Kandinsky, then the Montpellier Chapter (Swire Hotels, Hong Kong), and now it's the Malmaison. The Malmaison boutique hotel chain (17 hotels) was acquired in 2015 by the Frasers Hospitality Group, which is a branch of the immense Singaporean multinational real estate and property management company, Frasers Property.

Goodbye to the family hotel we loved!

Tony went on to work in the wine business, but later he combined his hotel experience with his love of oceans and distant places by working as a social host on cruise ships. He is the only one of us who still lives in Cheltenham, as does the youngest of his three children.

Robin Pagan became a minister of the United Reformed Church, and Gabrielle, besides raising their five children, helped with parish work and played the church organ. She later trained and then worked as a marriage guidance counsellor. They live in Diss, Norfolk.

The rest of us had never seriously considered a hotel career.

Heidi trained as a nurse, married Tony Fogarty, a doctor, had five children, adopted another, trained and worked as a teacher, remarried, loves being a grandmother, and together with her second husband, Chris Inman, a biomedical scientist, continues to foster children to this day. They live in Romsey, Hampshire.

Nicholas became an architect and later worked as a senior lecturer at Oxford Brookes University. He is the author of several books on research methodology. He is married to Ursula Mosele, a Swiss pianist from Lucerne, and they have three children. They now live in Bournemouth – but not in a hotel!

Susy trained as a teacher and taught in Birmingham and Nigeria before marrying a mathematics teacher and statistician, Ray Tongue. They lived in many different parts of the UK, and were active in many fields, but now seem settled in Saltdean on the south coast. They have three children.

New courtyard wing, Malmaison Hotel.

I worked in publishing before meeting the Swiss author Erhard von Büren and going to live in Switzerland, where I became a senior school French teacher. We married but don't have any children. We live in Solothurn.

No one in the extended family is working in the hotel business these days. Nevertheless, if my parents were still alive, they would be happy to see that they have twenty grandchildren and nearly thirty great grandchildren. The family they founded might not be a hotel dynasty but it's certainly not at risk of dying out.

Appendix
Letters and Newspaper Articles

The Blitz in London, November 1940

L ETTERS FROM MY FATHER in Kensington to my mother in Wales. (My translation.)

3 November 1940

[...] The last two nights were rather turbulent. The night before last, a bomb fell near Church Street. But by midnight everything was quiet again. Yesterday evening there was a strong wind, that the Germans made use of to set our neighbourhood on fire. For example, one fire started off in the courtyard behind the chemist's next to the De Vere Hotel [Hyde Park Gate]; an incendiary bomb fell on a balcony opposite, right next to the Broadwalk [in Kensington Gardens], another one further down the road. You remember the bomb that cut off our water supply? Down there the roofs of two small houses were on fire. In Victoria Road [the road behind the Prince of Wales Hotel] two bombs fell behind numbers 6 and 10. The Milestone Hotel got its third incendiary bomb. They had intended to get all the repairs done as quickly as possible and to open up again. However, this third bomb cut right through a water tank beneath the roof, and now everything is flooded. The manageress was all alone there. As you can imagine, she was near despair. What bad luck! First a fire, then another, then the blast from the bomb in the park, and now a 'baptism of fire'!

But the biggest conflagration last night was a bit further down than Kensington Court, in a big block of flats, you know, the large building opposite our bedroom. The flames shot up about twenty metres into the sky, sparks flew as far as us, and smoke came in all over the hotel. In the same direction but a bit further back, a garage was on fire. And on top of all this the wind was extremely strong and there was no rain. As you can imagine, I hurriedly and meticulously searched all the roofs and wells to see if we too had been gifted by Adolf. But we were lucky! While these fires were burning I was glad that no other bombers came. All this happened around 8.30 and was what you might call the 'spectacular finale'. We didn't have any high explosives in our area. The all-clear sounded at 11.30 and lasted till 7 the following morning. The night before, when the bomb fell in Church Street, there were ten parachute flares in the sky, five over Paddington, five over Victoria Station. They made a splendid sight, hanging like evening stars in the sky and drifting gently down to earth. [...]

8 November 1940

[...] During the last couple of nights the anti-aircraft guns were kept very busy and some alerts lasted fourteen hours. Last night, however, we had the all clear at 3 am – thanks to the morning fog. In spite of everything, I always go to my bedroom and sleep straight through the night. Quite strange! Then, the morning after, I hear from the others how awful the night was. At any rate, it doesn't seem to be a good idea for you to come back to London yet. [...]

16 November 1940

[...] Last night was lively again, not exactly pleasant, with rather a lot coming down. It was as bad as at the start of the Blitz when you were still here – you remember, those first bad nights. But I was in my room again, just going downstairs or to the watch upstairs from time to time to see if the walls on the other side of the building were still standing. However, from about three o'clock on I slept well in spite of everything. It so happened that the weather was very inviting for the planes, since the moon lit everything up as bright as day. The planes that drop the bombs here all seem to come over Hyde Park Corner or Marble Arch, never from the other direction. So I'm safer in my room than in the basement, as any bombs are more likely to hit the lower floors on the De Vere Gardens side than on the other. Never mind, in about three years the war will be over, cheer up! [...]

17 November 1940

[...] Now I'm back in my sitting room. Every afternoon at five, I get Beromünster [the Swiss national radio programme] very well on medium wave.

Last night was quite peaceful, I think we had the all clear shortly after one o'clock. Of course I didn't hear it. On the other hand, the night before last was awful. There are now two enormous holes in Kensington Park behind the Flower Walk, you know, where you used to sit in the shade of the trees with little Tony. In Gloucester Road, near the new block of flats, an oil bomb fell into the hole that was already there, but it didn't explode. Cornwall Gardens got a large bomb, Derry and Toms had one too, but it only got down as far as the third floor; St Mary's Hospital, the Savoy Hotel, Carlton Hotel; in Albemarle Street (near Brown's) between Piccadilly and Brown's there's a massive hole in the road, etc. etc. However, I slept very well in my room, but I think that if it gets so bad again I'll go downstairs after all, although I've got quite used to the whistle of bombs and the swaying of the building. I don't get nervous any more when I'm on watch. As to tablets, I haven't bought any yet, but I'll definitely do so if I get nervous again; or if I can't sleep – but there doesn't seem to be the least danger in that respect! [...]

Supper at the 1898 Cheltenham New Club Ball

E XTRACT FROM THE ARTICLE in the *Cheltenham Chronicle* of Saturday, 22 January 1898. (The flowers all came from 'Mr Cypher's nurseries'.)

NEW CLUB BALL CHELTENHAM

The Assembly Rooms never looked better than they did on Wednesday night, when this annual function, considered by many as 'the ball of the season,' took place. [...]

During the evening the company in relays took supper in the rooms upstairs, the beauty of which almost baffles description. In the centre of the first room was a "diamond" table, a pedestal in the middle of which supported an overtowering palm. Springing from this to the four corners of the table were floral arches, the lattice work of which was delicately and tastefully intertwined with orchids, tulips, lilies of the valley, ferns, and foliage. The table itself was covered with ornamental vases containing flowers both rich and rare, including cattleya, cypripediums, odontoglossums, lilies of the valley, etc. The rest of the room was occupied by a number of small round tables likewise decorated, and a large buffet, upon which George's Limited showed a vast array of good things. In the second supper room, the middle of the chief table was occupied by a lovely cocoa palm, the other tables being adorned with anthuriums, orchids, camellias, lilies of the valley, tulips, narcissi, etc. The beauty of Mr Cypher's floral decorations were [*sic*] the subject of comment among the numerous guests as they sat at supper. This was excellently served by George's Limited, according to the following menu:

HORS D'OEUVRE
Langue Crouté
Olives St. Augustine
*****

Saumon à la Royale

Escalope de Bécassine à l'Indienne
*****

Timbale de Foie-Gras aux Truffes
Mauviettes à la Belle-Vue
Cuisse de Poulet à la Parisienne
Côtelettes de Ris de Veau au Montpellier
Homard à la Maraicher
Salade de Tuica
*****

Pâté de Gibier à la Windsor
Hure de sanglier
[etc., with twenty-six further dishes, including turkey, pigeon pie, pheasant, capons, various trifles, cakes, creams and sweets – but no cheese.]

Decorations for the 1898 Cheltenham Bachelors' Fancy Dress Ball

EXTRACTS FROM THE ARTICLE in the *Cheltenham Chronicle* of Saturday, 5 February 1898. (The flowers were again supplied by 'Mr Cypher's nurseries'.)

CHELTENHAM BACHELORS' FANCY DRESS BALL
BRILLIANT CLOSE TO A SUCCESSFUL SEASON

Many who have attended this annual function for many years and some who can claim an acquaintance of more than 20 years were heard to declare on Wednesday night, when it came round once more, that the Assembly-rooms had never looked more pretty or artistic. [...]

Entering from the High-street through the carpeted corridor, the refreshment room was first reached. This was prettily draped in flutings of green and white sateen, the mirrors being held hidden in festoons of pale amber art fabric. A trellised archway, tastefully interlaced with trails of ivy and creepers, pointed the way into the crush room, the walls of which were concealed beneath a mass of pale green and rose pink flutings, the mirrors and doorways here being hung in pale pink, pretty baskets of flowers hanging from the centre. The corridor had been converted into three sitting-out rooms, the walls of which were hidden by varied but harmoniously blended shades of art muslin. The roof was hidden by balloonings of pale pink, the effulgence of the electric light being softened by pretty pink shades. The mirrors here, flanked on either side by palms, were festooned with variegated draperies, the beauty of which was enhanced by trails of ivy and a lovely display of flowers upon the mantels. The doorways leading into the ball-room were hung with plush curtains, but the hall itself presented a magnificent spectacle, especially when the gaily-moving crowd of whimsically-attired guests glided along the floor in time with the captivating music. The upper half of the large window was completely hidden by soft white draperies, which concealed the usual vallance and curtains. The lower half was in the form of an Eastern grotto, the three mirrors reflecting the beauty of Mr Cypher's floral display and the light from the candelabra hanging in front. In the middle of this and in other parts of the room were huge blocks of ice, which had an appreciable effect upon the temperature of the hall. The walls immediately above the large mirrors were completely hidden by a new style of drapery in pale lemon, contrasting prettily with the old style of festoons which prevailed in other parts of the room. Pale orange draperies overhung the fixed mirrors themselves, ingeniously looped by Cupids holding long trails of ivy, and showing up effectively under the light from the candelabra in front of each mirror. The pilasters were hidden in flutings of a new fabric of pale green tinsel, which gleamed prettily in the strong light thrown upon it. The balconies were also concealed by draperies of lemon and orange, the choice array of flowering and foliage plants beneath adding much to the charm. But the chief feature of all the bachelors' balls is the decoration of the gallery. Its usual appearance was transformed by trellised arches, which were interlaced with ivy and flowers, but above the gallery, rising to the ceiling of the hall, was a representation of the front of an Eastern residence, with four large window recesses, gracefully decorated with curtains of the prevailing tints and hanging baskets of flowers.

In such a scene as this the stewards […] attended to the comfort of their 420 guests, who from 10 to 3 tripped it merrily to the strains of the Royal Artillery Band, who in a style that could not be excelled took them through the following programme: [20 'Valses' interspersed with one Polka, two Lancers, a Pas de Quatre and, as a finale, a Galop]

The principal supper-room was also the theme of admiration by all, and deservedly so. As usual, the walls had been draped in the tints prevailing in the ballroom, but interest was naturally centred upon the tables. Here Mr Cypher had somewhat varied the style of decoration which has been in vogue during the season, and with good effect. The centre diamond table was adorned, not by the usual four floral arches, but by two three-span arches, charmingly adorned with orchids, lilies, camellias, etc. The other tables were also treated in effective style, both in this and the other supper rooms. George's Ltd. supplied the refreshments, providing an excellent menu and giving full satisfaction.

Subjoined is a list of the guests. It will be seen that many of the costumes were identical with those at the fancy dress ball a fortnight ago, but several innovations added a charm to the whole. Where no costume is appended to the name of the guests it may be presumed that they were in ordinary evening dress. [There follows a list of all the guests. About half of them were not in fancy dress.]

The Ladies' Bicycle Gymkhana

E XTRACT FROM THE ARTICLE in *The Cheltenham Examiner* of Wednesday, 18 May 1898.

Ladies' Bicycle Gymkhana

Charming weather, a large and fashionable company of spectators, pretty Lancer and exhibition riding, and spiritedly contested competitions combined to make the third annual Ladies' Bicycle Gymkhana, held at Montpellier Gardens on Monday, the most successful and enjoyable of the series yet given. Considering the earliness of the season, the promoters were particularly fortunate in that most essential condition to success in an out-door gathering – a bright and fine afternoon; while the performances of the fair cyclists were uniformly of so excellent a character that the interest of the spectators was well maintained throughout. The object which will benefit by the proceeds is the Nurse Fund of the Eye, Ear, and Throat Hospital. [...]

The programme opened with a "carousel parade of decorated bicycles". There were six entries of machines prettily adorned with flowers. Premier honours fell to Miss Annie Peatfield, the second prize to Miss Bubb, and the third to Miss Olive Cole. The first mentioned had artistically arranged arum lilies with lilac; Spain was depicted by Miss Bubb, who had introduced a representation of a bull fight on fan and bull's horns on the handle bars of the machine; and pansy blossoms were the predominant flower in Miss Cole's display. Among the other cycles was one rigged as a ship and displaying the Stars and Stripes intertwined with the Union Jack.

The competitions in skill commenced with a pole race, in which the eleven contestants were required each to drive a real polo ball down a course marked out with flags and make a goal, the quickest to achieve this object being the winner. [...] A display of cavalry sword drill, showing cuts, guards, and points, at Turk's heads, was the succeeding event. For this there were sixteen entries. [...] The Lancer musical ride (the Town Band occupying the orchestra), which followed, was a very pretty scene. Sixteen ladies took part, each attired in a white cycling costume, with straw hats, and bearing a lance with streamer. Directed by Colonel Lair, the various movements were performed with an ease and grace which elicited warm applause. The competitions were resumed with tent pegging. Armed with a lance, the cyclist in turn swept down upon a tent peg and lifted it out of the ground – at least, that was their task, and several succeeded in accomplishing it. [...] Another interesting contest was that of tilting at the ring – four rings to be taken off an erection about shoulder high with the lance. [...] Considerable skill was displayed by several ladies in the tortoise race (slow movement). [...] After a riding exhibition, the last event was commenced – a "consolation medley," in which tilting at the ring was combined with lance practice and tent pegging. The contest was a lengthy one, all except previous winners of first prizes being allowed to compete. [...]

At the close, the prizes were handed to the successful competitors by Mrs. de Freville, who was thanked for this act of courtesy by Mr. Wells, on behalf of the Committee. Mr. Wells also presented Colonel Leir, in the name of the competitors [twenty-three ladies], with the gift [a pair of silver candlesticks] which had been subscribed in recognition of his services as instructor.

CPSIA information can be obtained
at www.ICGtesting.com
Printed in the USA
BVHW030735250722
642887BV00016B/240

9 781914 407376